SIN
AND ITS
CONSEQUENCES

"But they that commit sin and iniquity, are enemies to their own soul."
—Tobias 12:10

SIN
AND ITS
CONSEQUENCES

By

His Eminence
HENRY EDWARD MANNING
Cardinal Archbishop of Westminster

Revised by TAN Books and Publishers, Inc.

"Now therefore saith the Lord: Be converted to me with all your heart, in fasting, and in weeping, and in mourning. And rend your hearts, and not your garments, and turn to the Lord your God: for he is gracious and merciful, patient and rich in mercy, and ready to repent of the evil."

—Joel 2:12-13

TAN BOOKS AND PUBLISHERS, INC.
Rockford, Illinois 61105

Originally published by Burns & Oates, London, and Benziger Bros., New York. Later reprinted by P. J. Kenedy, New York. No date was given on either edition.

This edition was edited and revised by TAN Books and Publishers, Inc. in 1986 from the P. J. Kenedy edition.

ISBN: 0-89555-299-X

Library of Congress Catalog Card No.: 86-50420

Printed and bound in the United States of America.

TAN BOOKS AND PUBLISHERS, INC.
P.O. Box 424
Rockford, Illinois 61105

1986

"Flee from sins as from the face of a serpent: for if thou comest near them, they will take hold of thee. The teeth thereof are the teeth of a lion, killing the souls of men. All iniquity is like a two-edged sword, there is no remedy for the wound thereof."

—Ecclesiasticus 21:2-4

"But if the wicked do penance for all his sins which he hath committed, and keep all my commandments, and do judgment and justice, living he shall live, and shall not die. I will not remember all his iniquities that he hath done: in his justice which he hath wrought, he shall live."

—Ezechiel 18:21-22

CONTENTS

Sermon I

THE NATURE OF SIN

"It is expedient for you that I go: for if I go not, the Paraclete will not come unto you; but if I go, I will send him to you; and when he is come, he shall convince the world of sin."

—John 16:7-8

Since last Lent began, how many souls that were gathered here have passed into eternity. And before another Lent begins, how many will stand before the Great White Throne. Who among us shall be the first to go to judgment? Let us, therefore, enter upon this Lent as if knowing it to be our last; let us begin this time of conversion to God as if we were sure that another would never be granted to us. "Bring forth, therefore, fruits worthy of penance, for now the axe is laid to the root of the tree; every tree, therefore, that bringeth not forth good fruit is hewn down, and cast into the fire." (*Matt.* 3:8, 10).

These thoughts have made me choose a subject, sad indeed and severe in all its parts, but vital to every one of us, necessary for our salvation, the root and foundation of all—I mean sin, its nature, its effects, its consequences. And I have chosen this subject because there can be none other so necessary, and because the precept of the Church, binding us all to Confession and Communion at Easter, begins more urgently to warn

1

the conscience of every member of the Catholic Church. I therefore appeal to you all. I appeal to your conscience to fulfill, each one of you for yourselves, this duty of salvation; and not for yourselves alone. Fathers and mothers, warn your families and households; friends and neighbors, warn with humility and charity all whom you know to be neglecting the practice of their duty to God.

The words of our Divine Saviour reveal to us what is the work and office of the Holy Ghost: "He shall convince the world of sin." Both in the old creation and in the new, both before the Incarnation of the Son of God and after His Ascension into Heaven, it has been, and it is, and it will be to the end of the world, the work and the office of the Holy Ghost to convince the world of sin; that is to say, to convince the intellect, and to illuminate the reason of man to know and to understand what sin is; and also to convict the consciences of men, one by one, of their sinfulness, and to make them, each one, conscious that they are guilty before God. This is the office of the Holy Ghost; and in all time, from the beginning of the world, the Holy Spirit of God has illuminated and convinced the intellect and the conscience of men to know God and themselves, and thereby to understand in some degree the nature of sin. But the fullness of that light and illumination was reserved unto the day of Pentecost, when the Holy Ghost came in person to dwell forever in the Mystical Body of Christ.

In the beginning, when God made man, He made him sinless, and He gave him the light of the Holy Spirit; so that man knew God, His holiness and perfections; and he knew himself, and the nature in which God had created him. He knew the law of God; but he did not know sin, because as yet the law had not been broken. He could not know it, because he had as yet no experience of the transgression of the law, with its bitterness and its fatal consequences; but when man sinned against God, then all was changed. Then he was conscious of his guilt, and strove to hide himself from the face of his Maker; but he only hid God from his own conscience. He could not escape from the presence nor from the eye of God; but he could hide the light of God's presence from himself—and this he did. Therefore, from the beginning of time, God in His mercy, by the working and light of His Spirit, taught men to know, in some measure at least, His own perfections and their own sinfulness; but it was only like the twilight preceding the noonday. We are in the noonday; and if in the noonday we are blind to the perfections of God and to our own sinfulness, woe to us in the day of judgment.

Therefore, my purpose is to begin by the most general outline of what sin is, and to lay down certain broad but simple principles which I shall have to apply hereafter in our future subjects. I therefore purpose first to speak of the nature of sin, of what it is, and of certain distinctions of sin, which will be necessary for us hereafter to refer to.

I. First, then, what is sin? There are many definitions of it, and one is this: it is the transgression of the law. "Sin is the transgression of the law." (*1 John* 3:4). God is a law to Himself; His perfections are the law of His own nature; and God wrote upon the conscience of man, even in the state of nature, the outline of His own perfections. He made man to know right from wrong; He made him to understand the nature of purity, justice, truth and mercy. These are perfections of God, and on the conscience of man the obligations of this law are written. Every man born into the world has this outline of God's law written upon him, and sin is the transgression of that law. Another definition of sin is: any thought, word, or deed contrary to the will of God.

Now, the will of God is the perfection of God Himself—holy, just, pure, merciful, true; and anything contrary to these perfections in thought, word, or deed is sin. The conformity of man to the will of God, to the perfections of God, is the sanctity or the perfection of the human soul; and the more he is conformed to the will of God, the holier and more perfect he is. Therefore, to be at variance with God is to be deformed; and the monstrous deformity of the human frame is not more humbling nor more hideous—nay, it is not humbling and hideous, compared with the deformity of the soul. When the soul is unlike to God, when it is departed from the perfection of God, when instead of purity there is impurity, instead of justice there is injustice, instead of truth there is falsehood, instead of mercy there is cruelty, instead of the perfections of God there is the direct contrary of those perfections: no deformity or hideousness that can strike the eye is so terrible.

The malice, then, of sin consists in this, that it is a created will in conscious variance with the uncreated will of God. God made us to His own image and to His own likeness; He gave us all that He could bestow upon us. He could not bestow upon us His own nature, because that is uncreated, and no creature can partake of the uncreated nature of God; but God could bestow, and He did by His omnipotence with His mercy, bestow upon us His likeness, His image, an intelligence and a will, a heart and a conscience, so that we become intelligent and moral beings. The malice of sin consists, then, in this: that an intelligent creature, having a power of will, deliberately and consciously opposes the will of its Maker. The malice of sin is essentially internal to the soul. The external action whereby the sinner perpetrates his sin adds, indeed, an accidental malice and an accidental increase of wickedness; but the essence, the life of the malice, consists in the act of the soul itself.

We see, then, that sin is the conscious variation of our moral being from the will of God. We abuse our whole nature: we abuse our intellect by acting irrationally, in violation of the will of God which is written upon the conscience; we abuse our will, because we deliberately abuse the power of the will, whereby we originate our actions in opposition to the will of God who gave it. We apply our intellect and will, with our eyes open and with freedom and choice, to the perpetration of acts, or the utterance of words, or the harboring of thoughts which are known to be contrary to the will of God; and, therefore, in every sin there is the knowledge of the intellect of what we are doing, the consent of the will in doing it, and the consciousness of the mind fixed upon the action despite these two objects: the law and the Lawgiver—the law of God known to us, and the Giver of that law, who is God Himself; so that we deliberately, with our eyes open and of our own free will, break God's law in God's face. Now, that is the plain definition and description of sin; and here I must, for a moment, turn aside from our path.

These last generations have become fruitful of impiety and of immorality of a stupendous kind; and among other of their impious and immoral offspring is a pestilent infidel school, who, with an audacity never before known in the Christian world, are at this time assailing the foundations of human society and of Divine Law. They have talked of late of what they call *independent morality.* And what do you suppose is independent morality? It means the law of morals separated from the Lawgiver. It is a proud philosophical claim to account for right and wrong without reference to God, who is the Giver of the Law. And what is the object of this theory? It is to get rid of Christianity, and of God, and of right and wrong altogether, and to resolve all morality into reason; and inasmuch as, it tells us, the dictates of human reason are variable all over the world, and change from generation to generation, this philosophy denies and destroys the foundations of morality itself.

Now, I should not turn aside to mention this monster of immorality and impiety, if it were not that at this time there is an effort being made in England to introduce under a veil this same subtle denial of morals, both Christian and natural. Only the other day I read these words, that "in the education of the people it is not possible, indeed, as things are, to teach morality without teaching doctrine; because the English people are so accustomed to associate morality and doctrine together, that they have not as yet learned any other foundation for morals." God forbid they ever should! The meaning of this is: Teach children right and wrong, but say nothing about God, nothing about the Lawgiver; teach them right and wrong if you will, but nothing about Jesus Christ. What is this but a stupidity as well as an impiety!

For morals are not the dead, blind, senseless relations that we have to sticks and stones, but the relations of duty and of obligation we have to the living Lawgiver, who is our Maker and Redeemer. There are no morals excepting in the relations between God and man, and between man and man. Morals mean the relations and duties of living and moral agents; and this *independent morality,* this morality without God for schoolchildren, is bottomless impiety if it be not the stupidity of unbelief. I could not help touching this in passing, and we will now go back to our subject once more.

II. I have now to draw two distinctions in the nature of sin. There are what are called formal sins, and what are called material sins. The importance of this distinction you will see hereafter.

1. Now, let us first understand what is a formal sin. It means a sin committed with a full knowledge of what we do, and a full consent to do it; so that in proportion as men have light, and know the law and the Lawgiver, in that proportion the sinfulness of their disobedience is increased. The holy angels were created by God in the full knowledge and light of His presence; and those who fell from their perfection by rebellion were formally guilty, in proportion to that angelic knowledge which left them without excuse.

All those who possess a clear light to know what is the law, and yet violate that law, are guilty, as Peter was guilty for denying his Master, and as Judas was guilty for selling Him; both were guilty in the proportion of their light. Those who, knowing the natural law, break that law, are guilty, because the law is written upon their conscience. Those who break the Christian law, knowing the Christian Faith, in the proportion of their light, are guiltier; and, above all men, those who have the full light of the Catholic Faith, if they break the laws of Jesus Christ, are the guiltiest on the face of the earth. You are guilty in the measure in which you have greater light; in the measure in which you have a fuller illumination, in that measure your guilt before God is greater.

Sins, then, are formal when committed with full light and consent. Now, what are material sins? The same actions done without sufficient knowledge, or without intention. Two men may commit the very same action, and the one be guilty before God, and the other not guilty. If, in the dark, I think that I am felling a tree, and with my axe I cut down a man, I am not a murderer. I have committed manslaughter in the dark, and without intention; and if the man I have slain be my own father, I am not a parricide; yet the act I have committed is materially an act of murder and of parricide. The quality of sinfulness, therefore, is purified, and taken away from the action, if I do not know what I am about, and if I do not intend it.

Our Divine Lord prayed for those who perpetrated the greatest sin that was ever committed on the face of the earth in these words: "Father, forgive them; they know not what they do." In His Divine compassion He prayed for His crucifiers; and the Apostle, speaking of Him, says: "Whom none of the princes of this world knew: for had they known him they would not have crucified the Lord of Glory." That is to say, among the multitude, perhaps the greater number did not know what they did, and that Divine prayer of compassion reveals a law of God's equity and pity upon the ignorant.

Nevertheless, those who know, or have it in their power to know, are guilty; for we are responsible not only for all that we do know, but for all that we could know, and therefore ought to know.

This is what you hear of as vincible or invincible ignorance. Ignorance takes away the guilt of our actions if that ignorance is invincible, for then we cannot overcome it. If we could not know any better, then God in His infinite mercy, though we have committed a material sin, will not take account with us as if it were a formal sin. But there is another kind of ignorance which is called vincible, because it may be overcome if we use the proper diligence to know; and God has put within our reach the means of knowledge sufficient if we will diligently seek it. Now let me apply these principles.

First. In the East there are churches which once were in communion with the Catholic Church, but have been for ages separated from it; and among those churches some have fallen from the Catholic Faith in respect to the doctrines of the Holy Trinity and the Incarnation. Generation after generation, millions have been born into that state; they never knew the perfect truth; they never were in the unity of the One Church. They believe that God has revealed Himself in Christianity, and they believe the doctrines they have been taught from their childhood to be that revelation. They believe God has a church upon earth, and they believe the church in which they find themselves to be that Church of God; and the simple, the unlearned, and those who have not the means of knowing better—we have every reason before God to believe in their good faith—live and die, and God in His mercy—we may also hope—does not take account of them as if they had the formal light to know the perfect truth. But to come nearer home.

It is to me a consolation and joy—I say it again and again, and more strongly as I grow older—to know that in the last three hundred years multitudes of our own

countrymen, who have been born out of the unity of the
Faith, nevertheless believe in good faith with all their
hearts that God has revealed Himself in Jesus Christ,
and that what they have been taught from their childhood is His revelation, and that He has founded upon
earth a Church, and that the Church, which in their
baptismal creed they call the Holy Catholic Church, is
the church in which they themselves have been baptized, reared, and instructed. It is my consolation to
believe that multitudes of such persons are in good
faith, and that God in His mercy will make allowance
for them, knowing what are the prejudices of childhood, of an education studiously erroneous, what is the
power and influence of parents and of teachers, of
public authority, and of public opinion, and of public
law: how all these things create in their minds a conviction that they are in the right, that they believe the one
Faith, and are in the one Church in which alone is
salvation. We rejoice to commend them to the love of
Our Heavenly Father, believing that though they may
be materially in error, and in many things materially in
opposition to His truth and to His will, yet they do not
know, and, morally speaking, many cannot know it,
and that therefore He will not require it at their hands.

2. This, then, is the first distinction of sin, into formal and material sin; yet I must draw one more, and
that is between Original Sin and actual sin. What is
Original Sin? It is the transgression of the law in the
head of the human race, whereby all who are born are
sinners before God, and born into a state of privation.
The transgression of the law in our head is *our* sin
because when God created man, He created mankind.
In that man the whole race of mankind was contained.
Mankind springs from one head, and that head was the

heir to all the benedictions of the kingdom of God in our behalf: our inheritance was contained in him. If he had stood, from him we should have inherited the kingdom of God; he fell, and by his fall disinherited the race of mankind. We hear men of this day say: "What can be more absurd than to believe that the human race fell because Adam ate an apple?" I put the words with all the bald impertinence of the world.

Let us see now whether the ways of God need justification. God created Adam, and placed him in Paradise in the midst of a garden. He gave him a dominion over every tree of that garden, except one only. Such was the generosity of God. He did not say: "Thou mayest eat of the fruit of that one tree, but of ten thousand other fruit-bearing trees of the garden thou shalt not eat; and in whatsoever day thou eatest of them thou shalt die the death." God did not, with the parsimony of a human heart, give Adam permission to eat of one tree, and forbid him ten thousand. No. He gave him free permission to eat of ten thousand, and forbade him to eat of one alone. Was there anything unreasonable in this? Was it not what you would do if you had the will to try the obedience of anyone? Was it not what you would do, and what men do at this day, when out of liberality they lease their lands upon what is called a peppercorn rent? When the world speaks impertinently, I may answer the world in its own tongue. The landlord who leases out his estate, taking only a nominal acknowledgment, is commended by all men as generous, large-hearted, noble-minded. He acts as a friend, without self-interest, when he entrusts to another man the enjoyment and enrichment which arise from his estates upon the mere acknowledgment that, after all, they belong to him. He is only reserving his right.

Now what did Almighty God in that commandment do? He reserved His right as Sovereign—He reserved His right over the obedience of the man whom He had created. He thereby revealed that He had jurisdiction over that garden, and over the man to whom He had permitted its free enjoyment. He put him upon trial—it was the test of his fidelity. More than this: it was a test so slight, that I may say there was no temptation to break the law. If he had been forbidden to eat of all the trees of the garden, save one, he would have been tempted at every turn. Every tree he gazed upon would have been a fresh temptation; he would have been followed and haunted by temptation wherever he went. God did not deal so with him—He forbade him one, and one alone; so that he had perfect liberty to go to and fro, gathering from the whole garden except from that one tree. Where, then, was the temptation?

As on God's part there was Divine generosity, so on man's part there was the wantonness of transgression. It may, indeed, be my defect, but I can see nothing in this that is not consonant with Divine wisdom, Divine goodness, Divine sovereignty, and Divine mercy. I see nothing to warrant the impertinence of the world. Well, this law was slight, and without any temptation whatsoever Adam transgressed it. He held the enjoyment of his perfection, and of the promise of eternal life, and of the kingdom of God, upon the payment, as I said before, of that quit rent, of that mere acknowledgment of the sovereignty of his Maker, and even to this he would not admit.

What, then, was the consequence? Man, as God made him, had three perfections. First, he was perfect in body and soul. Secondly, he had the higher perfection of the Holy Spirit dwelling in his heart, whereby his soul was ordered and sanctified, and the passions were held in perfect subjection to the reason and the will. Thirdly, he had a perfection arising from that higher perfection, namely, immortality in the body and perfect integrity in the soul. So that he had these three perfections: a natural perfection in body and soul, a supernatural perfection by the indwelling of the Holy Ghost, and a preternatural perfection of immortality; and all these by one act of disobedience he lost. When he sinned, the Spirit of God departed from him, his soul died because it was separated from God, his immortality was forfeited, the integrity or harmony of the soul was lost likewise, the passions rebelled, the will was weakened, the intellect became confused, and the nature of man was deprived of its supernatural perfection and of all that follows from it. This is the meaning of the words, "In the day thou eatest thereof thou shalt die the death." It was spiritual and temporal death, followed, except on repentance, by eternal death hereafter.

We see, then, the meaning of Original Sin in us. It is that we, being born of that forefather, are born disinherited of these three perfections which we lost in him by his disobedience. We are born into this world without the Spirit of God; we receive Him in our Baptism, which is our second birth. By our first birth, "that which is born of the flesh is flesh." We have the three "wounds," as they are called, of Adam—ignorance in the intellect, weakness in the will, and turbulence in the passions. This is the state in which we are born into this world, and therefore we are spiritually dead before God. I see in this, as I said before, nothing but Divine wisdom, and wisdom is justified of her children. And here I wish to answer what may perhaps arise in the minds of some of you concerning infants that die before Baptism. Sometimes people say, "How can I believe that those infants who die before Baptism, through no fault of their own, should go to eternal torment?" God forbid. Infants that die with Original Sin only, never having committed an actual sin—who believes that they descend into a place of torment? Their eternal state is a state of happiness, though it be not in the vision of God: for we know of no way in which any human soul can see the vision of God except by regeneration of the Holy Ghost.

Without receiving the grace of Holy Baptism, the soul is not in the supernatural order; and of those who die in the natural order we are unable to affirm that the grace which belongs to the supernatural order is extended, and that, because for this we have no revelation. It is, however, certain that the privation attached to Original Sin carries with it nothing which the world, sometimes contradicting the Christian Faith for the purpose of maligning it, most unreasonably says against it. But though Original Sin is only punished by privation, every actual sin will be punished by actual pain. There is pain of sense which follows actual sin; every actual sin that men commit will be punished by pain, either temporal or eternal, for pain follows sin as the shadow follows the substance.

Lastly, we come to actual sin. What is it? Let us recall the principles with which I began. Actual sin is the conscious variance of a creature to the known will of its Creator; and that conscious variance includes the light of the intellect, and the consent of the will, and the knowledge and intention of what we are doing. The essential malice of sin is in the will: and there is a threefold malice in every actual sin committed by a Christian. First, there is a malice against God the Father, who made man to His image and likeness, that He might be the object of his love; that he might love Him, know Him, serve Him, worship Him, be conformed to Him, and dwell with Him in eternity. The Christian who sins against God sins against his Creator, and worships the creature more than the Creator; that is to say, worships the world, his pleasures, himself. Self-worship he puts in the place of the worship of God, and in that he does an infinite offence—infinite, though he be finite—because the Person against whom that offence is committed is an infinite God.

Secondly, there is a malice against our Lord Jesus Christ, the Redeemer of the world. The Apostle says every sinner is "an enemy of the Cross of Christ." He says, "They that do such things, I have told you often, and now again tell you weeping, that they are enemies of the Cross of Christ." (*Phil.* 3:18). And why? Because Jesus Christ suffered on the Cross for those very sins which such men commit. The sinner nails Him on the Cross once more. The nails and the hammer were but the material instruments of crucifixion; the moral cause of the Crucifixion of the Son of God was the sin which you and I have committed; and if we commit such sins again, we deliberately renew the causes which nailed Him on the Cross. Again, the Apostle says, if those who despised the law of Moses were condemned, of how much severer punishment shall he be thought worthy who hath trodden under foot the Son of God, and put Him to open shame, and counted the Blood of the Testament, whereby he was sanctified, unclean; and hath done this in despite to the Spirit of Grace! (cf. *Heb.* 10:28-29).

The Christian who deliberately commits sin wounds our Divine Saviour. He opens those Five Sacred Wounds, making them bleed afresh. With a cold and ungrateful heart he renews the sorrows which caused the agony of Gethsemane, and made Our Lord sweat His Sweat of Blood.

Not only this; but thirdly, there is a malice against the Holy Ghost. Every sin that is committed, is committed against the light and grace of the Holy Spirit in the conscience; and in this there are three degrees. We may grieve the Holy Ghost, we may resist the Holy Ghost, and we may quench the Holy Ghost. Our Divine Lord has said, "Every sin and every blasphemy shall be forgiven unto men, except the blasphemy of the Holy Ghost; and if any man shall speak a word against the Son of man, it shall be forgiven him; but whosoever speaketh against the Holy Ghost, it shall never be forgiven him in this world nor in the world to come." (*Matt.* 12:31-32). Now what is the meaning of this? A man may speak against Jesus Christ, ay, blaspheme his Lord; and the Holy Spirit, convincing him of sin, may bring him to repentance, may convert him to God, and his soul may be saved; but any man who commits mortal sin and refuses repentance, thereby blasphemes the Holy Ghost, who is the Spirit of Penance, the Spirit of Absolution, the Absolver of the penitent. Such a sinner rejects the whole dispensation of grace; and, therefore, the sin that shall never be forgiven is the sin of impenitence. Every sin that men repent of shall be forgiven; but the sin that is not repented of shall never be forgiven, neither in this world, nor in the world to come.

In giving these definitions, I am afraid that what I have said is somewhat abstract, perhaps somewhat tedious; but it is impossible for me to make clear what I have to say hereafter, without laying down first principles. I will now, therefore, only make application of what I have said. We have here two practical principles.

1. The first is this: no one is so blind to his own sins

as the man who has the most sin upon him. If a man is plague-stricken, he can see it by the discoloration of the skin. If the scales of leprosy are coming up upon his arm, he can tell that he is a leper. If a cloud is growing over the pupil of the eyes, he can tell that he is losing the light of heaven. All the diseases of the body make themselves known emphatically; but it is the subtilty and danger and deadliness of sin that it conceals itself. No men know the light of God's presence so little as those who are covered with sin; and the more sin they have upon them the less they can see it. Though all the perfections of God, like the rays of the sun which encircle the head of the blind man, are round about them all the day long, they are unconscious of His presence. They are like Elymas, the magician, who, for his impiety, had scales upon his eyes; and because they do not see the light of God, therefore they do not see His perfections, and therefore they do not see themselves; for the light of the knowledge of self comes from the light of the knowledge of God. How shall a man know what unholiness is, if he does not know what holiness is? How shall he know what falsehood is, if he does not know what truth is; or impurity, if he does not know purity; or impiety, if he does not know the duty we owe to God, and the majesty of God, to whom worship is due? Just in the proportion in which the light of the perfections of God is clouded, we lose the light of the knowledge of ourselves; and the end of it is that when men hear such words as I am speaking now, they say, "That is just the character of my neighbor—that is the very picture of my brother"; they do not see themselves in the glass. You may describe their character, and they will not recognize it; you may tell them, "This is yourself," and they will not believe it. There is something

within them which darkens the conscience; and why is
it? Because sin stupefies the intellect and the heart: it
draws a veil and a mist over the brightness of the intelligence, and it darkens the light of the conscience.
Sin is like hemlock: it deadens the sense, so that the
spiritual eye begins to close, and the spiritual ear
becomes heavy, and the heart grows drowsy. And when
men have brought themselves to that state by their own
free will, then comes the just judgment of God: "I will
give them eyes that they may not see, ears that they
may not hear, hearts that they may not understand, lest
they should be converted, and I should heal them.
These things said Isaias, when he saw his glory and
spoke of him." (*John* 12:40-41).

2. There is one other truth—that no men see the
nature of sin so clearly as those who are freest from sin;
just as no intelligence knows sin with such an intensity
of knowledge as God Himself. Our Divine Lord Jesus
Christ, the sinless Son of God, knew sin in all its
hatefulness so as no other human heart has ever known
it. His Immaculate Mother—because sinless—knew the
sinfulness of sin by the light of her intelligence, and by
a pure horror of her whole spiritual nature. So in like
manner the saints of God, each one of them in the proportion of his sanctity; and so you likewise, in the
measure in which you are free from sin, in that measure
will you hate it, in that measure you understand and
estimate its sinfulness. And if at any time in your life
you have committed sin, in the measure in which you
are separated from your past life—in the measure in
which that old character of yours has been taken off
and you can see "the old man" which you have
sloughed off, that old being and nature of yours which
cleaves to you no longer, which you look on as a thing

hideous and horrible, belonging to you no more, belonging to your childhood, boyhood, or youth, but yours no longer now—in that measure you understand the sinfulness of sin.

You can look back on your past life, and understand your sins as you did not understand them then; and when you come to die, your present character and your present life will be seen by you in a light, brighter and more intense than that under which you see them now. Look up, therefore, into the light of God's presence, and pray God to make you to know yourselves as He knows you, and to see yourselves as He sees you now; for when you have seen the worst of your sins, what are they, compared with those which God sees in you? Therefore, do not let us ever think that we know all our sins; do not let us imagine that we fully know our own sinfulness. We are only beginning to learn it, and we shall have to learn it all our life.

There are three great depths which no human line can sound—the depth of our sinfulness, the depth of our unworthiness, and the depth of our nothingness. If you are beginning to learn those three things, happy are you. Be not afraid, the more you see your own sinfulness; and for this reason. Who is showing it to you? It is the light of the Spirit of God. It is He who alone searches the heart, who alone makes us know ourselves; and the more you see of your own sinfulness, the truer pledge you have of His presence; that He is with you, that He is within you, that He is busied about your salvation. He is giving you a pledge and a promise that every sin you see He will help you to repent of, and every sin you repent of shall be washed away in the Precious Blood of Jesus Christ.

Therefore, one last word. My first counsel to you in

this Lent is this: Try to know yourselves, try to learn during these days such knowledge of yourselves as you have never had before. Begin as if it were for the first time. Take the Ten Commandments: read them in the letter; understand them in the spirit; and try your life from your childhood, from your earliest memory, by that Divine rule. Take the seven deadly sins, try yourselves by them, in deed, in word, and in thought. Pray to the Spirit of God, whose work and office it is to convince the world of sin. Pray every day in this Lent, morning and night, that the Spirit of God may illuminate your reason to understand the nature of sin, and convince your conscience, that you may know what sins are upon you. Pray to Him that the light of the presence of God may come down upon you like the light of the noonday, that you may see not only the broad outlines of your sins, but your finer and more delicate and more subtle offences against God, even as we see the motes which float in the sunbeam at noonday.

The more you have the presence of God with you, the more the light of His perfections is upon you, the more you will see yourselves. The Patriarch Job, who, though he had long lived in prayer, in converse and in communion with God, and had been grievously afflicted (which more than any other discipline brings men to know themselves)—nevertheless, at the end of all his trials, when God spoke to him out of the light of His presence, said: "With the hearing of the ear I have heard thee, but now mine eye seeth thee; wherefore I condemn myself, and do penance in dust and ashes." (*Job* 42:5-6).

Sermon II

MORTAL SIN

*"Being filled with all iniquity, malice, fornica-
tion, avarice, wickedness, full of envy, murder,
contention, deceit, malignity, whisperers, detrac-
tors, hateful to God, contumelious, proud,
haughty, inventors of evil things, disobedient to
parents, foolish, dissolute, without affection, without fidelity, without mercy. Who, having known
the justice of God, did not understand that they
who do such things, are worthy of death; and not
only they that do them, but they also that consent
to them that do them."*

—Romans 1:29-32

Our next subject is mortal sin. But before I enter
upon it, I wish to recall to your memory the general
principles already laid down. First, we know that the
end of man is God; that God made man for Himself;
that He made him to His own likeness; that He made
him capable of knowing, loving, and serving Him, and
of being like to God; and that in the knowledge, the
love, and the service, and the likeness of God, is the
bliss of man. Therefore, conformity to God is our perfection, and union with God is eternal life; but deformity, or departure from the likeness of God, is sin, and
separation from God is eternal death. The nature of sin
is, as we have defined it, the transgression of the law of

God; or, in other words, any thought, word, or deed deliberately committed with the knowledge of the intellect, and the consent of the will, contrary to the will of God; or, in other words again, it is the variance of the created will against the Uncreated Will—of the will of the creature against the will of the Creator. The essential malice of sin, then, consists in the variance of the will of the creature against the will of his Maker. These were the principles which I laid down last time. We will now take them up again, and make application of them in one particular point.

But first I shall bring forth the distinction of the Apostle St. John between that sin which is "unto death" and that which is "not unto death." The Apostle wrote, "he that knoweth his brother to sin a sin which is not to death, let him ask, and life shall be given to him, who sinneth not to death. There is a sin unto death: for that I say not that any man ask. All iniquity is sin. And there is a sin unto death." (*1 John* 5:16-17).

Now what does St. John mean by contrasting *sin unto death* with sin *not unto death?* The difference cannot be the same as between sins that are called *mortal* and *venial,* for he says that if a man ask, that is, if a man pray for his brother who has committed a sin that is *not unto death,* life shall be given him: therefore such a one had lost the life of grace and had been guilty of a mortal sin. And when the Apostle speaks of a sin that is *unto death,* and adds these words: "For that I say not that any man ask [for forgiveness for the sinner who commits this sin]," it cannot be supposed that St. John would say this of every mortal sin, but only of some heinous sins which are very seldom remitted, because such sinners very seldom repent.

Now St. John, in these words of his epistle, tells us

that if any man see his brother sin a sin which is not unto death, he ought to pray for him. Now, what are the sins that are not unto death? They include sins of infirmity; sins of impetuosity; sins of strong temptation; sins which by the subtlety of Satan leads men astray; sins of passion, in which human nature, being weak and tempestuous, and liable to disorder, is drawn aside: if in all these there be not that malice which refuses to repent. Now, these are sins which all Christians are liable to commit, and do commit, and which, without doubt, you yourselves are profoundly conscious of committing. These are sins not unto death, as we may trust, because, if there be not an impenitent malice against God or our neighbor, then the soul might yet return to God through repentance; and in that case, St. John says, "Let him pray for him, and God will give life unto those that sin not unto death"; that is to say, He will give grace, sorrow, pardon, help, protection, and perseverance. He will watch over those souls if in humility and in sorrow they persevere; and the prayer of those who are faithful and steadfast will obtain grace for those that sin not unto death.

Then he goes on: "There is a sin unto death: for that I say not that any man should ask": that is, that any man should pray for forgiveness for such a sinner. Now which sins are those which are *unto death*? By a sin that is *unto death* is commonly understood a willful apostasy from the Faith and from the known truth, when a sinner, hardened by his own ingratitude, becomes deaf to all admonitions, will do nothing for himself, but runs on to a final impenitence. The sin of Judas was, as far as we can see, a sin unto death. With his eyes open, with a knowledge of his Master—though, perhaps, he did not know of the mystery of the Incarnation as we know it now; nevertheless he knew enough—he sold his Master, and yet, perhaps, not knowing that he sold Him to be crucified; and then, despairing, he went out and hanged himself. This, then, was a sin unto death.

The sin of apostates from the Faith,[1] who, having known the truth, and having had the full light and illumination to know God, afterwards fall from Him, is described by St. Paul in the Epistle to the Hebrews, where he says, "It is impossible for those who have been once enlightened, and have tasted the Heavenly Gift, and of the good Word of God, and of the powers of the world to come, if they shall fall away, to be renewed again to repentance." (*Heb.* 6:4-6). All those who, having had full light and knowledge of God in His revelation, turn from it with their eyes open—of whom St. John says, "They went out from us, because they were not of us; for if they had been of us, they would no doubt have remained with us" (*1 John* 2:19)—those who so sin, sin unto death, and are left to the judgment of God.

The "sin against the Holy Ghost," which "shall never be forgiven," is a sin unto death. This comprises sins that embody a stubborn resistance to the inspirations of the Holy Ghost and His work in the soul, and an open contempt for His gifts. These sins are six: despair of one's salvation, presumption of God's mercy, resisting the known truths of faith, envy of another's spiritual good, obstinacy in sin, and final impenitence. Although no sin is absolutely unpardonable, those who sin against the Holy Ghost stubbornly resist the influence of grace and do not wish to repent. Hence their sin cannot be forgiven them.

Thus such sins are so often accompanied by the sinner's hardening of his soul against repentance that St.

John gives little encouragement to such as pray for these sinners to expect what they ask. In one word, all who are impenitent sin unto death.

Now our faith teaches us from the holy Scriptures that God desires not the death of any sinner, but that he be converted and live. (*Ezech.* 33:11). Though men's sins be as red as scarlet, they shall become as white as snow. (*Is.* 3:18). It is the will of God that everyone come to the knowledge of the truth, and He left a power in His Church to remit the most enormous sins; so that no sinner need despair of pardon, nor will any sinner perish but by his own fault.

For those who sin unto death, St. John in these words does not forbid us to pray; he says, "I do not say"—that is, "I do not enjoin it." He leaves it to the conscience of every man. He says of those who sin not unto death, that we have all confidence we may obtain pardon and grace for them; but for those who do sin unto death, we have no such confidence, and, therefore, though he does not enjoin it, he does not forbid it.

St. John does not say that such a sin is never remitted, or cannot be remitted; he only says: "for that I say not that any man ask" for remission: that is, though we must pray for all sinners whatsoever, yet men cannot pray for such sinners with such a confidence of always obtaining their petitions as St. John had described previously, in verse 14: "And this is the confidence which we have toward him: that whatsoever we shall ask according to his will, he heareth us."

Then he goes on to say, "All iniquity is sin." Now, iniquity means all departure from the rectitude of God and of the law of God. Iniquity is inequality, or crookedness. Everything that is not conformed to the rectitude of God, to His perfections, to His law, and to

His will, is sin. "And there is a sin unto death."

Now it must be stated that every mortal sin is a *sin unto death* inasmuch as it immediately drives sanctifying grace from the soul and causes the supernatural death of the soul. Furthermore, if the soul should die in that state, not having repented according to the law of God, it would go to Hell, and that one mortal sin would thus have proven to be a sin unto eternal death. But since God will forgive any sin, no matter how grave, if the sinner come to Him in repentance through the Sacrament of Penance, the commission of mortal sin need by no means end in eternal death; rather, it should be followed by contrition, confession, the forgiveness of God and the return of sanctifying grace, penance and eternal salvation. Thus the Apostle distinguishes between those mortal sins which involve impenitence and those which do not involve impenitence.

As I have said before, to constitute any sin it is necessary that the man who commits it should know what he does—there must be a knowledge of the intellect; if not, the sin is only, as I then said, a material sin, and not a formal sin, unless his ignorance be a culpable and guilty ignorance. Next, he must not only know that he is doing wrong, but his will must consent to the wrongdoing. And, he must know and consent deliberately, with such an advertence or attention to what he is about as to make him conscious of his action. A man who should transgress the law of God in the least possible way would fulfill these conditions.

Now there is a distinction between mortal sin and venial sin; the latter is lesser sin, which does not cause the death of the supernatural life of the soul. It would be a transgression of the law of God if I should take an apple off the tree of my neighbor without his leave. It was his: I had not a right to take it, and I thereby broke the commandment, "Thou shalt not steal"; but that certainly would not be a mortal sin. The "taking of an apple" in the Garden of Eden became a mortal sin when a divine prohibition was laid upon such an act under pain of death, and that the pain of eternal death; but where there is no such command laid under pain of death, it is quite clear that the taking of an apple would not constitute a mortal sin. Therefore it is necessary that there should be gravity in the matter of the sin—otherwise the sin is venial, not mortal.

Now the gravity of that matter will be constituted in one of two ways—it is either the material gravity, that is, the extent, or amount, or quantity of the sin committed; or it is the moral gravity derived from the circumstances of the case. An illustration will at once make this clear.

If I were to rob a man of a very large amount of his property, no one would doubt for an instant that I had committed a mortal sin. The common sense of mankind, the instincts of justice, would at once pronounce against me. But if I were to take a needle from some rich person, the instincts of justice would acquit me of a mortal sin. I would have taken that which did not belong to me, but no one would say that in taking that needle from the rich man, who could obtain an abundant supply of needles, I had committed a mortal sin. No. But suppose that needle belonged to a poor seamstress, who gained her daily bread by the industrious use of that one needle, and that she had not the means to buy another; and that if she were robbed of it, her industry must cease, and she could no longer gain her bread; and that I knew all those facts; and that, with my eyes open, knowing the extent of the in-

jury I was doing, in violation of the law of charity, as
well as of the law of justice, I should take that needle
with a perfect consciousness that I was destroying her
means of industry and reducing her to hunger. You see
at once that there is a moral guilt which arises from
these circumstances. Suppose, still further, that I myself
were jealous of her prosperity, being of the same trade
or calling, and that I took the needle in order to ruin
her for my own advantage. You see, therefore, that in
so small a theft as the stealing of a needle there may be
an enormity of moral guilt.

It is not enough to constitute a mortal sin, then, that
there should be the knowledge of the intellect and the
consent of the will to the action; the matter in which
that action is committed must be of a grave kind, either
materially or morally, before God.

There are seven capital sins, the names of which you
all know. These constitute man's main ways of committing sin; they are the source of all other human failings.
(They are not necessarily always mortal sins.) First of
all, there is pride, which separates the soul from God;
secondly, there is envy, or jealousy, which separates a
man from his neighbor; thirdly, there is sloth, which is
a burden pressing down the powers of man, so that he
becomes weary of his duty towards God, and forsakes
Him; fourthly, there is avarice, which plunges a man
deep into the mire of this world, so that he makes it to
be his god; fifthly, there is gluttony, which makes a sen-
sual fool; sixthly, there is anger, which makes a man a
slave to himself; and, lastly, there is impurity, which
makes a man a slave of the devil. In those seven kinds
there are seven ways or routes to eternal death; and all
those who, with their eyes open, with the knowledge of
the intellect, and the full consent of the will, commit sin

in any of those seven kinds, are walking in the way towards eternal death.

1. We come now to the effects of mortal sin. The first effect of one mortal sin, as we said before, is to strike the soul dead. The grace of God is the life of the soul, as the soul is the life of the body; and one mortal sin, in any one of the kinds that I have spoken of, strikes the soul dead. The soul dies at once, and on the spot; not as the tree which is blasted by the lightning and dies gradually, day after day: first in the leader, then it begins to die in the branches, and then it dies in the trunk, and then it dies in the root. That is a slow process, but it is not so with the soul. One single mortal sin strikes the soul dead at once, and that for this reason: the grace of God is the life of the soul, and one mortal sin separates the soul from God.

The holy angels, when they were created, lived in the presence of God, though they did not as yet see the face of God. They were on probation. Every creature depends on God in two ways: he needs the support of God for his existence; and of the grace of God for his sanctification. If God were not present with us at this moment in our physical life, we should die. If He were not in this building, the walls of it would vanish. So it was with the angels in their first state of bliss. It was the assistance of God which sustained them in their being as pure intelligences, spotless in their innocence, excellent in their strength, surpassing in their energy. "He maketh his angels spirits, and his ministers a flame of fire." (*Heb.* 1:7). They also needed grace. The angels were holy just as we are holy, because the Holy Ghost was with them; and all the supernatural actions of the angelic perfection were sustained by an actual grace of God, just like our own. By one sin—one mor-

tal sin—and that a sin of pride, purely spiritual, they
fell and died eternally and without redemption (change
of mind or repentance is not possible to the angelic
nature), and, as St. Jude writes, "Leaving their habita-
tions, were cast down into darkness and everlasting
chains until the day of judgment." (*Jude* 1:6).

As it was with the angelic natures, so it was with
man. God, when He created man, constituted him, as I
said before, with three perfections—the perfection of
nature, that is, of body and soul; the supernatural perfection, or the indwelling of the Holy Ghost and of
sanctification; and the preternatural perfection or the
perfect harmony of the soul in itself, and the immortality of the body. These three perfections, natural,
supernatural, and preternatural, make up what is called
original justice; and in that state man was constituted
when he was created. But by one sin of disobedience,
with his eyes open, with the consent of his will and with
full deliberation—and that in a matter light in itself, as
I have said, but grave because the prohibition of God
under the penalty of eternal death was laid upon it—in
that slight trial, without temptation save only the listening to the tempter, who awakened a spirit of curiosity
and disobedience, in a place where all around him
everything was permitted and one only thing forbidden,
man sinned against God, and by that one sin was struck
dead. The Holy Ghost departed from him, and all his
perfections were wrecked. The supernatural perfection
was lost, the preternatural perfection was forfeited, the
soul fell from God, the body was eventually struck by
death. Man became from that time disinherited, shorn
of sanctity and life: one mortal sin had separated him
and all his posterity from God. But unlike the angels,
Adam was able—with the help of God's actual grace—

to have contrition and to repent. And as it was in the case of Adam, so it is also in the case of the regenerate; so it is in our own. We who are born into the world spiritually dead have once more, by regeneration in Baptism, the life of the Spirit. But if we sin mortally, with our eyes open and with consent of our will, we forfeit the presence of the Holy Ghost in the soul, the supernatural Charity (love) of God which unites us to Him, the sanctifying grace whereby we are made children of God, and the seven gifts of the Holy Ghost which are always inseparably united to His presence.

Yes, Charity leaves the soul when sanctifying grace leaves. There is left in us, indeed, supernatural Faith and supernatural Hope. These two remain like the beating of the pulse and the breathing of the lungs: there is just so much left of the life of grace—the light of Faith and the aspiration of Hope after God (though even Faith leaves the soul if a man commit the sin of unbelief; and Hope leaves the soul with the commission of the sin of despair, and by the sin of unbelief). But our union with God is broken: we are separated from Him, and at variance with Him. This is the first effect of mortal sin; for habitual grace (sanctifying grace) and the presence of God are the life of the soul; and the loss of that grace, which is the loss of the presence of God, is the death of the soul.

2. But further: one mortal sin destroys all the merits that the soul has ever heaped up. Understand what is meant by merit. The doctrine of the Catholic Church is this: not that any creature can merit in the sense of claiming out of the hand of his Maker, Redeemer, and Judge, by any right of his own, anything whatsoever in nature or in grace. Cast out of your minds forever all shadow of misunderstanding upon this. Merit does not

signify that the creature can by any right of his own, either in the order of nature or of grace, challenge and demand of God the gift or the possession of anything. No. The word "merit" is used in two senses. There is the merit for good, and the merit for evil. Every good action bespeaks a certain conformity to the will of God, and will merit a reward; and every evil action bespeaks a deformity, which will merit, or be followed by, punishment. Therefore, "merit" is a word altogether indifferent in itself, and derives its meaning for good or for evil from its context.

Merit for good, according to our faith, signifies the connection or link that exists between certain actions done in the state of grace, and certain awards; and that connection or link is constituted sovereignly and gratuitously by the gift and promise of God. So that every man who does acts of faith, or of charity, or of self-denial, or of piety, will receive a reward—both in this life and the next—according to those actions. Every man who does acts of charity will receive an increase of charity and of grace in this life; and hereafter, as the Council of Florence defines, the glory of the blessed shall be in proportion to the measure of their Charity on earth.

There is a link, then, between the measure of our Charity here and the measure of our glory hereafter. This is what is called merit; and all through our life, if we are living faithfully in the grace of God, we are thereby heaping up merits, and acquiring in virtue of the promise a greater reward and a greater bliss. I may give as example the life of the Apostles, who, through the whole of their career, even to their martyrdom, were continually increasing in the sight of God the accumulation of His grace, and of His reward—including the reward of salvation itself. This is true of you all, and through your whole life everything that you do according to the will of God, being in a state of grace, has in the Book of Remembrance a record, and in the Sacred Heart of our Divine Master a promise of reward, which shall be satisfied at His coming.

One mortal sin, then, unless afterwards repented of, utterly cancels all these merits of a whole life. It matters not how long you may have been living a life of justice, of charity, of humility, of generosity, and of piety, before God—one mortal sin, and the whole of that record is canceled from the Book of His remembrance. It is all gone as if it had never been.

Do you need proofs of it? Take the history of David, the "man after God's own heart." (*Acts* 13:22). You remember his faith, his patience, his fidelity, his courage, his prayer, his spirit of thanksgiving. He is the Psalmist of Israel, the man with the greatest of all titles— "the man after God's own heart." But in one moment, by the twofold sin of murder and adultery, he canceled before God every merit of his youth and of his manhood: all was dead before God. Solomon, the son of David, the type of our Divine Lord, the King of Peace, the man famous for wisdom—not only because he received it as a divine gift, but because he had the wisdom to ask for wisdom, not for riches—the man illuminated beyond all other men, because afterwards he fell away from God into mortal sin, all the merit of that long life of wisdom and light and of early sanctity was canceled.

Judas, in his childhood, and in his boyhood, and in his youth, was perhaps as faithful to the light of his conscience as you have been. He left kindred and all that he had, to follow his Master. No doubt there were in his heart struggles and aspirations and prayers and desires to walk in the footsteps of his Divine Lord; but there crept upon him the sin of covetousness. He carried the bag, and that which was put therein; and Satan tempted him, and then entered into him, and he sold his Master.

Ananias, in like manner, renounced the world, periled his own life to become a Christian, sold all that he had, made sacrifice of everything; but fraudulently kept back part of the price. Demas was the companion of Apostles, and exposed his life to danger, and lived in toil and poverty and perpetual risk, the companion of the Apostle of the Gentiles until he forsook him, having loved this present world (*2 Tim.* 4:9); and all the merits of that life of faith, and of all those actions which once were recorded in the Book of God's remembrance, were in one moment canceled; and therefore St. Paul said of himself, "I keep under my body, and bring it into subjection, lest, after I have preached the Gospel to others, I myself should become a castaway." (*1 Cor.* 9:27). The prophet Ezekiel says, "When the just man shall turn away from justice he hath done, and shall commit iniquity; in the iniquity he hath done, in the sin he hath committed, in that he shall die, and his justice shall be no more remembered." (*Ezech.* 3:20).

3. The third effect is even more terrible; it mortifies and kills the very power of serving God. All the actions of a man in a state of mortal sin are dead; they have no merit or power to prevail before God for his salvation. So long as he is separated from God, nothing he does has saving power. Just as a tree that has life bears living fruit, and a tree that is dead has nothing but fruit that is withered and dead, likewise a soul that is planted in God, as we all are by Baptism, strikes its root as the tree by the rivers of water, and increases continually in Faith, Hope, and Charity, and in the seven Gifts of the

Holy Ghost, which expand themselves like the leaves upon the branch, and the twelve Fruits of the Holy Ghost unfold themselves and ripen.

On the other hand, a soul that is separated from God is like the tree that is cut asunder at the root; and as the severed tree withers from the topmost spray and every fruit upon it dies, so the soul in the state of mortal sin— even if it be only one mortal sin—so long as it remains in that state, is separated from God, and can bear no fruit unto salvation. The Apostle has declared this in the most express words: "Though I speak with the tongues of men and of angels, and have not charity, I become as sounding brass and a tinkling cymbal; and if I have all prophecy and all knowledge, and can understand all mysteries, and though I have faith and could remove mountains, and have not charity, I am nothing; and though I give my goods to feed the poor and my body to be burned, and have not charity, it profiteth me nothing" (*1 Cor.* 13:1-3)—that is to say, a soul separated from God, that is, not in the state of grace and thus not having the gift of Charity, the love of God. It matters not what the soul may know; it may be able to prophesy, to expound mysteries, to work miracles: it may give all it possesses to the poor in alms, it may be martyred, as men may think, and yet, if it hath not the love of God, it profits nothing to salvation.

There will be at the last day those who will come to our Divine Lord and say, "Lord! Lord! we prophesied in thy name, we cast out devils and did many mighty works in thy name; we have eaten and drunk in thy presence"; and He will say unto them, "Depart from me, I never knew you" (*Matt.* 7:22, 23): that is to say, a soul that has lost the life of grace by one mortal sin, one transgression, continuing in that state, until re-

stored to union with God by grace and Charity, is dead
before God, and all the actions of the soul are dead.

Those who are in such a condition are like men looking up to a high mountain on which the sun dwells perpetually in its splendor, and there is a glory as of the
Heavenly City upon it, and they long to climb up to it;
but before them there is the breast of a precipice,
which no human foot can scale, and they pine away
with longing and with the impossibility of ascending: or
they are like men gazing upon a fair country, the Promised Land of vineyards and olive yards and fig trees,
and rivers flowing with milk and honey, and homes of
peace are before them; but at their feet there is a river,
so deep and rapid, without ferry and without ford,
which the mightiest swimmer cannot pass. So it is with
sinners. The law of God stands between the soul that is
cut off from Him, between the soul that is out of grace
and the peace of God.

4. And not this only: the soul in itself begins to lose
its vigor and its strength. As I said before, every
creature needs the help of nature and of grace; and the
supernatural gifts of God—Faith, Hope, and Charity—
are by a mortal sin either entirely destroyed or
weakened. Charity is utterly destroyed. Hope remains
and Faith remains, but Hope begins to grow faint; for a
man conscious of having sinned mortally against God
cannot deceive himself with the hope of salvation
unless he has grounds for hope; and what grounds can
an impenitent sinner have? The Faith that remains in
him—what does it show to him? "The Great White
Throne," "the smoke that ascendeth up before the Seat
of Judgment," the law of God written in letters of fire:
"There is no peace, saith my God, for the wicked" (*Is.*
48:22), and "without holiness no man shall see the

Lord." (*Heb.* 12:14). Faith shows him judgment to come, and the witnesses that will stand before the Throne on that day and bear testimony against him; and therefore the Faith that remains in him is a terrible light, warning him and piercing his conscience. So far the supernatural Faith that is still with him is goading him with fear to bring him back to God; more than this it cannot do.

The natural powers of the soul are also affected when a man is in a state of sin. The heart becomes corrupt, the soul becomes weak. Let me take what may seem to be an example not fitting for you. You who listen to me are not likely to be tempted to excess, or intoxication, but it is an apt example to illustrate every kind of sin. The man who indulges himself in drink loses the vigor and command of his will. The will becomes feeble and loses its imperious control. It can no longer command the man. It is like a rotten helm which the ship will not obey. The will itself becomes paralyzed—there is a solvent which has been eating away its elasticity and its power, and what happens in this gross example happens in every other. I might take falsehood, sloth, or other sins I named before—but you must make application for yourselves. The very will loses its power of repenting.

Ay, and there is a still more terrible thought than this. Sometimes the sins that men have committed long ago are the cause of their instability, their inconsistency, their wavering and irresolution at this day. They have never yet returned to God; they have never yet been really restored to the grace of God and vitally united to Him. They carry within them that which we read of in the Book of Job, where it says: "His bones are full of the vices of his youth, and they shall go down with him to his grave." (*Job* 20:11).

5. Lastly, there is another effect of mortal sin; that is, that it brings a man into a double debt before God—it brings him into the debt of guilt, and into the debt of pain—and he will have to pay both. The debt of guilt he must answer at the Day of Judgment. The debt of pain he must suffer before he can see God, either here, or after death in the state of purification: or else he will suffer in Hell to all eternity. Every substance in this world has its shadow. You cannot separate the shadow from the substance. Where the substance moves the shadow follows; so every sin has its pain; it matters not whether we think of it or no, whether we believe it or no. So it is: God has ordained it from the day in which He said: "In the day that thou eatest thereof, thou shalt die the death." From that day onward, no sin has ever been committed that has not been followed by its measure of judicial pain. It must be someday expiated, either by bearing it here or bearing it hereafter, or by a loving sorrow prevailing with God through the Precious Blood of Jesus Christ, to wash out from the book of His remembrance the great accumulated debt of pain from sin.

I will not go further into these effects; I will only sum up what I have said. First of all, one mortal sin strikes a soul dead, driving out from it the Holy Ghost, sanctifying grace, and Charity. Secondly, one such sin destroys all the merits of a long life, be they what they may; hereafter I will show how they may all revive again, like the spring after the wintertime—but this, not for the present. Thirdly, one such sin mortifies, kills, and destroys the saving power of every action that the soul may do while in that state of separation from God. Fourthly, it weakens both the supernatural elements that remain in the soul (the virtues of Faith and Hope), and the natural powers and faculties of the soul itself. Lastly, it brings the soul into the double debt of guilt and pain. These are the five effects of a mortal sin—a sin which will surely take the sinner down to Hell, to eternal death, unless he repent.

I have but a few words of counsel to add. The first is this: meditate every day of your lives upon this great and awful truth—how easy it is to fall from God; and say to yourselves, "God is my end; for Him I was created—and if I fall short of that end by a hair's breadth, if I swerve aside from attaining that end, I shall go down into eternal death." An arrow shot at a mark, striking a hair's breadth aside from its aim, fails to attain it. A ship steered by a confident and cunning hand, if it miss the light, is wrecked, be it ever so near the port: and a soul that does not attain to union with God here in a state of grace will be separated from God to all eternity. Next say to yourselves, "If I do not correspond with the grace which God has given me, I shall miss my eternal end." As I have before said, God is cooperating with every creature. The drawing of His Holy Spirit, and the gifts of His grace, are like a chain of gold drawing every created soul to Himself. "God wills all men to be saved, and to come to the knowledge of the truth"; and again, our Divine Lord has said: "And I, if I be lifted up from the earth, will draw all things unto Me."

God is drawing every created soul to Himself. He is drawing them to the knowledge of Himself and of His Incarnate Son, and of the Precious Blood shed on the Cross from the Sacred Heart of Jesus; and the graces and the love and the breathings of the Holy Ghost are perpetually going out and drawing souls to Himself,

and to the Unity of the Church. God is always drawing
souls to repentance, and through repentance to perfection, and from one degree of perfection to another, raising them higher and higher to union with Himself. This
is always going on, but we must correspond with it.
Listen to Him, respond, answer, lay hold of that grace
which is offered to you, keep fast the links of that
golden chain, never let it go, and take heed lest you
break its links.

We often think, if a soul that is already in eternal
death could once more return, what would be the fervor
of such a soul through all the time granted it on earth.
What humility, what hatred of sin, what holy fear of its
occasions, what piety, what self-denial, what self-
sacrifice, would mark a soul that once had tasted eternal death, if it could return, and have one more opportunity of salvation. What a life of the Cross, and of intense devotion to God, that soul would live! You have
never yet gone down into eternal death. You have been
the subject of a greater grace than even if you had been
liberated. You are still in life, still surrounded by the
light of truth; you have yet the graces of the Holy
Ghost in abundance; you have time; you have opportunity; you have the seven Sacraments; you have the
Holy Sacrament of the Altar, the Precious Blood of
Jesus Christ: all that is needful for eternal life—ay, and
that in abundance, without stint and without measure.
You are perhaps even like the Prodigal Son before he
left his father's house—you have not yet tasted that far
country, and the guilt and misery of falling from God.

Therefore, say to yourselves: "God be praised! for I
am still in life, and my day of grace is not gone by."
The sun is yet in the heavens; with some it is in the
morning still, with others it is the noontide, with some

who hear me it is declining towards the horizon. Say: "Lord, abide with us; for it is towards evening, and the day is far spent. Give me grace to make my peace with Thee, that I may be united with Thee, lest Thou find me parted from Thee in the day of Thy coming."

This, then, is the first thought I would pray you with all my heart to make day after day; and the other is like unto it, but it is more terrible. Day after day say this to yourselves: "If I fall from God—as I easily may—I shall go down alive into Hell."

Dear brethren, we live in days when men must speak plainly. There are among us, going to and fro, as there are in foreign countries, mockers, scoffers, blasphemers, ministers of Satan, apostles of lies, who say there is no Hell. Eternal punishment? Medieval fables! Popish superstition! True it is that the Church which is called "Popish" inflexibly maintains that there is a Hell, that there is an eternal punishment, and that they who live and die impenitent will go down alive into that torment. It is a glory that such a charge is laid against the Church of Rome. I accept the accusation—ay, and as a minister of Jesus Christ, and as an apostle of His Gospel, I declare that God has revealed that there is hereafter eternal pain and everlasting death. As there is a Heaven, so there is a Hell.

As there is eternal life, so there is eternal death. Be on your guard, then, dear brethren. Be not so shallow or so credulous. Let no impostors, who pretend to philosophy and to criticism, lead you for one moment to believe that the existence of Hell and eternal punishment is by an arbitrary law, by a mere act of Divine legislation, like a statute made by despotic power. Eternal death is an intrinsic necessity of the perfection of God, and of the willful sin of man. If there be a God

who is holy, just, pure, true, and unchangeable; then, if
man is impure, unjust, unholy, and false, and will not
change by repentance, then as light and darkness cannot exist together, God and that soul cannot unite in
eternity. It is not a statute law. It is an intrinsic
necessity of the Divine perfection on the one hand, and
of the sinfulness of the human soul upon the other.
Why is the human soul unholy and unjust? By the
abuse of the free will which God has given us—as I
said in the beginning—by the open-eyed transgression
of God's law, by the deliberate breaking of His commandments, by the impenitent persevering in that state
of disobedience and of separation from God, which in
itself is death, which is eternal death in time, which is
Hell upon earth. Except the soul repent, it already
begins to taste the condemnation of eternity.

Therefore, bear in mind that the holiness of God and
the sinfulness of man are enough clearly to demonstrate
the intrinsic necessity of an eternal separation. And
what is Hell but to be separated from God eternally—
and to be separated from God not as we are here, with
our souls clogged and stupefied by sin, intoxicated by
the world, ignorant of ourselves! No. After death, the
eyes of the soul will be opened, the scales will fall from
its sight, it will see itself for the first time, as it will for
the first time see God in judgment. And when it shall
see God in judgment, all that instinct of the soul in
which it was from the beginning created for God, an instinct like the needle of the compass, which points by
its own law always to the north—as in the blaze of the
noonday, so in the darkness of the midnight—will
return to its direction. The lost soul that was created in
the image of God, of which the beatific end is God—
and to be united with God is life—will then begin to

hunger and thirst after God, when to be united with God is impossible forever. Just as breathing is a vital necessity to the body, so union with God is a vital necessity to the soul.

You know sometimes in sleep a sense of stifling and suffocation in which you seem to lie an endless night in torment; conceive to yourselves an eternity of that suffocation, when the soul is conscious of the vital necessity of its union with God, when to be united with God is eternally impossible. Ay, more than this, there will be a torment in the soul which is the undying worm that will gnaw to all eternity. What is that torment? Remorse. The consciousness that the soul has committed self-murder, that it died because it sinned unto death, and that it sinned unto death of its own free will. There was no constraint, no necessity. With its own free will it sinned against God, and broke the link of union with Him. In eternal death the worm that dieth not, the perpetual tooth of remorse, will make the soul conscious of an anguish which no human heart can conceive. There is no need of fire to torment; this alone is torment enough, to lose God eternally; to have eternal remorse without anything more is Hell—but there will be more. Those who are lost will be lost together—multitudes, myriads of millions—all in misery, all separated from God, all in remorse, all feeding on themselves, hateful and hating one another.

I have not said one word as yet of that which I now will add. It is true there is a Divine mystery which we shall know—God grant not by experience. Our Divine Lord has said it: "Where the worm dieth not, and the fire is not quenched." And again: "Go, ye cursed, into everlasting fire, prepared for the devil and his angels." There is an eternal pain by fire. God has declared it.

Woe to the man that denies it! Satan is always endeavoring to efface this belief out of the minds of men—doing everything he can by subtle philosophy, by specious reasoning, by appeals to the mercy of God, by wonderful exaltations of the Divine perfections, and criticisms upon the Greek Testament, by laughter, derision, scoffing, and mockery, before which many a man who is not afraid of going into battle is coward enough to run away. Satan is always endeavoring to root out the belief of eternal fire from the minds of men. I will tell you why. Because the greater multitude of men have so little hunger and thirst after God, so little aspiration after union with Him, that they are conscious only of the fear of an eternal pain to keep them from sin. If Satan could only efface from the minds of men the thought of eternal pain, there is nothing left to restrain them; and for this he is always laboring.

There is nothing Satan loves better than to get men to laugh at him, to use his name in jest, to interlard their conversation with some reference to him in mocking levity, which very soon makes men cease to fear him, and then cease to believe in his existence. On the other hand, God is always striving to awaken and revive in the conscience of each one of us the sense of the danger of eternal death, by His Divine Word, by the voice of His Church, by the whispers of conscience. He is perpetually reviving in every one of us the sense and belief that there is hereafter a judgment and a condemnation to eternal fire.

Live, then, as you would wish to die; because as you die, so you will be to all eternity. Precisely that character which you have woven for yourself through life by the voluntary acts of your free will, be it for good or be it for evil, that will be your eternal state before God. If God find you clothed in the white raiment which is the justice of the saints, happy are you; you will walk before Him in white forever. If you be found in the rags and tatters of the Prodigal before his repentance, you will be cast out from His face, and all men will see your shame. As you live, so you will die; as you die, so you will be forever. God is unchangeable. You are continually changing; but death will precipitate the form in which you die, and you will be so fixed forever. As the tree falls, so it shall be. Make one mistake, and that mistake is made forever.

Oh, dear brethren, look round about us; how many men there are that are learned, and scientific, and noble, and eloquent, and prosperous, whom the world honors! How many there are that are amiable, and loving, and loved, and their neighbors think no evil of them; they see nothing but the fair outside—the whited disguise. Some one mortal sin—God knows what—unrepented of, is within. Whited sepulchers—fair without; within, full of dead men's bones, and of uncleanness. Dear brethren, that may be our case. Say to yourselves, every one of you: "That may be my case—that may be my likeness before God at this moment." "It is appointed unto all men once to die, and after that the judgment." (*Heb.* 9:27). And hear what that judgment will be: "I saw a great white throne, and one sitting on it, before whose face the heaven and earth fled away, and there was no place found for them; and I saw the dead, small and great, standing in the presence of the throne, and the books were opened; and another book was opened, which was the book of life, and the dead were judged out of the things that are written in the books, according to their works . . . and death and hell were cast into the pool of fire, which is the second death; and whosoever was not found written in the book of life was cast into the pool of fire." (*Apoc.* 20:11-15).

NOTES

1. In our secularized times, when apostasy or abandoning of the Christian religion is so common and is taken so lightly, we need to realize the terrible seriousness of this sin, the gravity of this insult to Almighty God. Yet the Church does not forbid apostates to return to the Fold; rather, she absolves them in the Name of Jesus Christ and welcomes them back if they return to God in true repentance in the Sacrament of Penance. We can be certain that God desires our prayers and sacrifices for the return of these lost sheep. Parents and godparents, in particular, should persist in praying for the return to the Faith of any of their children who have left it. The Blessed Virgin Mary is especially powerful in winning souls back to God, and it is to be remembered that at Fatima Our Lady particularly pointed out that "God grants graces through the Immaculate Heart of Mary."

Sermon III

VENIAL SIN

"For a just man shall fall seven times and shall rise again."

—Proverbs 24:16

"For in many things we all offend. If any man offend not in word, the same is a perfect man."
—James 3:2

There is a distinction between sins which cause the immediate death of the soul, and sins which do not; or, in other words, sins that are mortal, and sins that are venial—a distinction not spun out by the subtleties of theologians, but written broadly in the Word of God. Last time I spoke of mortal sin; it remains for me now to speak of the sins that are not mortal. The sum of what I said last time is this: that mortal sins are deadly, for that they separate the soul from God. God is the life of the soul, and a soul separated from God is dead. A soul separated from God in this world, unless restored to union with God in this world, by the operation of His grace and of repentance, will after the death of the body be separated from God for all eternity. Such is the second death, or in other words, Hell.

I drew out the reasons to show the existence and the necessity of Hell—that Hell, or the loss of God forever, is in strict truth the perpetuity of the state of separation

from God which the sinner has freely chosen for himself in this world, so that Hell is linked by an intrinsic
necessity to mortal sin; that the separation of the soul
from God through mortal sin results, by an intrinsic
necessity, from the unchangeable perfections of God on
the one hand, and the obstinate variance of the created
will against God on the other; and that, therefore, every
soul that dies eternally dies by self-murder. It is not
more a just judgment pronounced at the bar of a future
tribunal than an intrinsic necessity of that state to
which the soul has freely reduced itself.

This is the sum of what I have already said; and I
now go on to those sins which are not mortal, or which,
in the common language of theology, are called
"venial." The word "venial" is used here in the sense of
"pardonable"; venial sins are those which may be pardoned. In a general sense, there is only one sin which
cannot be pardoned—that is, the sin that is not repented of. Every mortal sin that man commits—if repented of—may be pardoned: "Every sin and blasphemy shall be forgiven, except only the blasphemy of the
Holy Ghost[1] . . . That shall never be forgiven, either in
this world or in the world to come." (*Matt.* 12:31-32).
And therefore in one sense, and that a general sense
only, every mortal sin is in a sense "venial" if con-
sidered in this way: that it may be pardoned to the true
penitent through the Precious Blood of Jesus Christ.

But the technical sense of the word "venial" is something precise and distinct. It means those sins which
may be found in souls that are united with God, and are
in the grace of God, and in the love of God, and in a
state of habitual obedience. This needs to be more
carefully explained; and I am conscious that in explain-
ing it I ought to distinguish between venial sins and

temptations, but time will not now suffice. I must hope hereafter to find an occasion on which I may speak of the subject of temptation as distinct from sin. Therefore, I intentionally set it aside at present.

The sins which may be found even in men in the state of grace are sins of lesser matter; or, they may be sins committed without full knowledge or consent. They are often sins of infirmity committed through weakness; or sins of surprise committed by sudden or strong temptation; or sins of impetuosity, where passion carries a man for a moment beyond self-control; or sins of indeliberation, that is, done in haste, before as yet conscience and the reason have had time to deliberate and weigh what they are about; or, lastly, they may be sins committed with some degree of deliberation.

Now, the seven capital sins, as they are called—anger, pride, gluttony, impurity (lust), ambition (avarice), jealousy (envy), and sloth—these seven are the capital sins, under which almost every kind of sin may ultimately be reduced; and of those, six at least may be venial. The seventh is one in which, if any man sin deliberately, with his eyes open, and with the consent of his will, he can hardly be free from mortal sin, because lightness of matter cannot be supposed in that instance to exist—I mean sins against the holy virtue of purity. But sins of anger, of pride, of gluttony, of ambition, of jealousy, of sloth, are susceptible of degrees and shades and distinctions with regard to gravity of matter; and they may be also committed, as I said before, through infirmity, through surprise, through impetuosity, and without deliberation, and even with some degree of deliberation, without being mortal. This will explain what we read in Holy Scripture: "The just man falleth seven times." "Who can understand sins? From my secret faults cleanse me, O Lord." (*Prov.* 24:16; *Ps.* 18:13).

It is clear that even the saints of God, through infirmity, and through temptation, have offended against God, and yet they have not broken their friendship, nor separated their souls from Him. For example, all those who preserve their baptismal innocence are in a state of union with God, and all such will be saved. They are united with God through the indwelling of the Holy Ghost; they are children of God, and if they die they will most assuredly inherit the kingdom of Heaven. Nevertheless, all those who preserve their baptismal innocence—and I trust that many who hear me have never lost it—are conscious while they hear me of the multitude of personal faults—ay, and it may be habitual faults of temper, of ambition, of jealousy—of which they are guilty. Is there anyone here who will venture to say he is not conscious of some besetting sin, of some—ay, perhaps of many, faults—and yet he may still be in the grace of his Baptism; and of this we may believe our Lord spoke when He said: "He that is washed hath no need save to wash his feet, but he is clean every whit." (*John* 13:10). That is to say, he has been cleansed in the Precious Blood of Jesus Christ in Holy Baptism, therefore those lesser or venial sins are washed away by sorrow, by contrition, by mortification, and by absolution. (Venial sins can be forgiven even outside the Sacrament of Penance.)

Once more. I will suppose that a man has fallen from his baptismal grace; and that through a true conversion and a real and solid repentance he has returned to God. Perhaps some who hear me are in this state. They are conscious that they would rather lay down their lives than offend God again, in the way in which they had offended Him before; nevertheless they are perfectly conscious of a multitude of faults against God and their neighbor; and yet those faults do not prevail to break their union with Him, nor to turn away the friendship of God from them, and they have not relapsed into their former state.

We are, in fact, like soldiers in warfare: wounded, and spotted and spattered by the blood of the conflict. We are laborers out in the field, and the soils and stains of our toil cleave to us. We are wayfarers in the road, and the dust settles upon us even when we do not know it. We cannot go out of the world and the world's evil. We are in contact with it, and it casts more than its shadow upon us. It casts its stain, and the stain abides.

The most perfect machine, constructed with the most faultless accuracy, if it be jarred by a shock, is at once thrown out of gear, it loses its perfect action, and its motions become eccentric. So it is with human nature. It was created perfect—in the image of God, with the three perfections, natural, supernatural, and preternatural, of which I have spoken already; but by the shock of the Fall it was thrown out of gear. It became eccentric, it lost its rest upon God, its true center, and it began to turn faultily round itself. The three wounds of the soul—ignorance in the intellect, turbulence in the passions, weakness in the will—are the injury done to that perfect machine. Wherefore, continually our nature is acting abnormally, that is, in departure from the law of its Maker. This seems to be the Apostle's meaning when he says: "I know that in me—that is, in my flesh—dwelleth no good thing. For to will is present with me; but how to perform that which is good I find not. For the good that I would, I do not; but the evil which I would not, that I do. Now if I do that which I would not, it is no more I that do it, but sin that dwelleth in me. But I see another law in my members, warring against the law of my mind, and bringing me into captivity to the law of sin which is in my members. Unhappy man that I am, who shall deliver me from the body of this death?" (*Rom.* 7:18-24). These were the words of the Holy Ghost by the Apostle, and this is precisely what I have been describing. The Apostle was a saint of God, in union with God, in friendship with God; but he was conscious that in himself there was a perpetual warfare, a turbulence in his nature, a weakness in his will; yet those sinful emotions, passions, and temptations were not sins: only an act of consent could make them sins in the sight of God. [2]

We are approaching, then, an understanding of venial sin. It is a transgression of the law of God; a thought, word, or deed, at variance with the will of God, in a matter that is not grave, or in a grave matter but without full knowledge or without full consent. This will suffice to distinguish the sin which is venial from that which I described last time, where with eyes open and willing consent, in a grave matter, a sinner breaks the law of God in the face of God. What I have now to point out are the consequences of venial sins.

It is quite true they do not break our friendship with God; but do not for one moment deceive yourselves by thinking that venial sins are what are called little sins. There is no such thing as a little sin. Before I have done, I hope to convince you that all sins are great, even those that do not destroy the supernatural life of the soul. The consequences, then, of venial sins are these:

1. First, venial sins diminish the grace of God in the soul. When theologians say that venial sins diminish

grace, they always make this distinction—they do not mean to say that the quantity of the grace of God is made less, because the grace of God is like life, which cannot be diminished. We are either alive or dead; but the living powers may be diminished. Life remains, but the health and the vigor and the strength of the living man are lessened. Therefore, the diminution of grace means that it diminishes the fervor and the operation and energy and efficacy of grace.

St. Bernard says that fervor—that is to say, the life of fidelity and obedience—has many effects; and two of those effects are these: First, it renders whatever we have to do easy to us; and, secondly, whatever we do easily, we do with pleasure, and find a sweetness in it. They know this who have learned to speak a foreign language, or to use a musical instrument. Nothing is more tedious, repulsive, or trying, than the acquisition either of a foreign language or of the practice of music; but the moment we have attained a certain facility in either, there is a sweetness in exercising that acquired skill; so that we are ready at all hours to practice it, and at every moment we have a sensible enjoyment in making use of the acquired faculty.

Now, it is just so with obedience, with prayer, with mortification, which is the most repulsive of all things to our nature. They who use self-denial and mortification grow to love it, and find a sweetness in it; but the moment they begin to indulge venial sins of any sort or kind, they begin to lose that sweetness. The moment they begin to commit venial sins of worldliness, of vanity, of self-indulgence, the palate becomes vitiated, the taste is spoiled. The pure spiritual taste, which makes self-denial and prayer sweet to them, loses its purity, and the world's excitement, pleasure, vanity, flattery, incense, and the like, become sweet; and as these things become sweet, the facility of prayer and self-denial is lost, and they become difficult. A repugnance to them grows up; they are done with effort; they are postponed; they are limited; they are restricted; they are reduced to a minimum; and, finally, the fervor of the soul is lost.

What, then, is fervor? It does not mean emotion. Fervor consists in the firm desire and effectual resolution to fulfill our duties to God with these three things: regularity, punctuality, and exactness—that is, doing our duty to God by rule; doing it punctually at the right time; and exactly, that is, as perfectly as we can. But if we have been indulging venial sins of any sort or kind, we begin to do our duty towards God in a slovenly way; we neglect the right time; we do it irregularly; we put God off with an imperfect service. Those venial sins are like the dust settling upon the perfect machine of which I spoke. As the dust accumulates upon the timepiece, the motion of the timepiece becomes slower; and as it becomes sluggish it loses its perfection. So again, as I said, mortal sin is the death of the soul—but venial sin is the disease of the soul. Those who willingly allow themselves to fall into such infirmities and imperfections, which are not yet mortal, are like men who are making bad blood—men in whom morbid humors are accumulating; a lingering malady is upon them, through ill-using the vigor of their life. This is the first effect.

2. We are always receiving sufficient grace from Almighty God, who, in His infinite mercy, "maketh his sun to rise upon the evil and the good, who sendeth his rain upon the just and the unjust." (*Matt.* 5:45). There is a perpetual flood and inundation of the grace of God,

coming down upon the whole race of mankind; but most especially upon those who are in the light of His Faith, and in the unity of His Fold. Well, the effect of these venial sins, these personal faults—I will not again go into a detailed account, you must individually examine your hearts, and make application—the effect of these sins is to hinder the reception of grace, to shut grace out. The Apostle says, "We are not straitened in him, we are straitened in ourselves." (*2 Cor.* 6:12). If our hearts were as large as His hand, we should be filled with His grace; but our hearts are narrow. The hands of Almighty God, which are infinite, are perpetually pouring out grace upon us. It is like the rain that comes down upon the sand of the shore, or upon a hungry sea, or upon the stony mountains.

There are two ways that we are continually receiving grace: the one way is in the Sacraments; the other, out of the Sacraments. The grace we receive in the Sacraments is of two kinds. Every Sacrament gives sanctifying grace, and also a specific sacramental grace (which is actually a special aspect or function of sanctifying grace). In Baptism, the sacramental grace is spiritual rebirth, by which we are made children of God: "the grace of adoption whereby we can cry Abba, Father" (*Rom.* 8:15); moreover, it is the grace whereby we are enabled to fulfill all the duties that belong to the children or to the sons of God. This is the meaning of St. John when he says, "To as many as received him, to them gave he power to be made the sons of God." (*John* 1:12). That is, every baptized person has grace from the time of his Baptism to fulfill every duty of the love of God and of his neighbor, every duty of piety towards God, every duty of obedience; so that at no time in his life—childhood, boyhood, youth, or manhood—will he ever fail of doing his duty towards God from any lack or denial of grace on God's part. But those who, having received the grace of Baptism, as I have said, in this twofold sense, begin from early childhood with all manner of little faults, and grow up to boyhood and youth with faults growing stronger and stronger, and more and more in number, yet perhaps not arriving at mortal sin—such men are continually choking, stifling, keeping down the working of grace within them.

So, again, in the Sacrament of Penance. Those who have come to the Sacrament of Penance in mortal sin, and therefore without the love of God, and unable to bring with them any sorrow except the sorrow of fear and hope, do receive in the Sacrament the grace of Charity; that is, the love of God is restored to them when they receive back sanctifying grace. Afterwards they are able to make the acts of contrition perfect in kind, though not perfect in degree, and fulfill all the duties of a penitent; but if they begin to return to their venial sins, to give way to their infirmities, impetuosities, and temptations in the manifold kinds I have described, the spirit of penance, contrition, and humility is hindered and lasts but a little time.

Once more. Perhaps one of the phenomena of the spiritual life most to be wondered at is this: that whereas one Communion worthily made, in which we receive the Precious Body and Blood of Jesus Christ, is enough to make us tabernacles of the Holy Ghost and saints, there are those who go to Holy Communion every week, and perhaps every day, and, to our shame, there are priests of God who every day offer the Holy Sacrifice, and receive the Precious Body and Blood of our Lord, and yet are not saints. It is a miracle of our insensibility and earthliness that we should be what we are, and yet be daily holding in our hands the Holy Sacrifice of the Body and Blood of Jesus Christ. Why is all this? The sacramental grace of the Holy Eucharist is the abundance of the outpouring of Our Lord's Holy Spirit, which accompanies the Holy Sacrament as the rays of the sun go with the sun. Where the sun is, the splendor of his presence is besides; and if our hearts were not narrow and cold, and choked by a multitude of faults and infirmities, we should be so filled by one Communion that we should be elevated from the low level on which we are to a life that is far above us.

Next, there are the graces outside of the Sacraments. There are lights by which God makes the soul to know His truth, and by which He draws the soul to His presence. We read in Holy Scripture: "When thou hast said, Seek ye my face; my heart said, Thy face, Lord, will I seek." (*Ps.* 26:8). Such is our answer; but it is a ray of light from Him. It is a ray of the light of Divine truth and of the Divine grace, which speaks to the intellect and the conscience. If we would open our intellect with sincerity to receive the light of truth, and our conscience to receive the attraction of Divine grace, it would fill and illuminate us; but by faults of self-indulgence, worldliness, fear of man, and human respect, we bring a film over our eyes, and the inward eye of the intellect and conscience at last loses its faculty of discernment. Its sight is confused, like men who have what is called color-blindness. They cannot distinguish colors, they put red for green, and green for red; and so some people "put light for darkness, and darkness for light, and sweet for bitter, and bitter for sweet," as the Prophet says; that is, confusing together the grace of God and the inspirations of nature.

We all are between two attractions; there is the attraction of God, and the attraction of the world; and without breaking with God, there are multitudes who are living under the play and influence of the world. They would not break with God for anything that could be offered, even for the world and all contained therein; nevertheless, they would not break with the world, and they try to do that impossible thing—that is, to "serve God and Mammon." Thus they are in the condition of which our Lord speaks, when He says: "Behold, thou art neither cold nor hot. I would thou wert cold or hot; but because thou art neither cold nor hot, but lukewarm, I will cast thee out of my mouth." (*Apoc.* 3:15-16).

3. Thirdly, another consequence of venial sins is that they dispose the soul for mortal sin. Just as ailments and slight sicknesses are the forerunners which pull down the strength and render men susceptible of greater diseases, so lesser sins prepare the way for greater. It is like, I may say, the heaping up of fuel.

Let me take as an example what we call a smoldering temper. People who are irascible and tempted to anger, though for a long time they fight against it, afterwards begin to indulge it, and to allow the smoldering temper to go on like a charred beam in a house, which may smolder for months before the fire breaks out. Some day there comes an occasion when a temptation meets that smoldering temper, like letting air in on the burning beam; and the whole soul is in a blaze, and malice, or hatred, or resentment, or revenge breaks out.

Again, there are such things as pattering lies, little insincerities, slight swervings from truth. The world is full and the atmosphere of the world is thick with those insincerities. They may not be mortal, they may be venial, they may be little lies of courtesy, little false-hoods of excuse; but the day comes when this perverse habit of not speaking the exact truth has so confirmed itself upon the tongue and upon the will, that upon an occasion in which a man would have cut off his right hand rather than have told a lie, he will tell a lie boldly, and will stand to it. He has been long laying up the fuel for this sin. Once more—but this is an example which I postpone, because I shall have to speak of the subject more fully—little negligences and omissions prepare the way at last for the mortal sin of sloth.

More than this, these venial sins have the effect of giving a perverse inclination to the will. If in winter-time the rain descends upon the unfinished wall of a house, soaking through to its very core, and if then there come a frost, the frost makes the wall swell, and it loses its perpendicular. The winter has been a still winter, and the snow has fallen and the wind has not risen. At last comes the wintry wind, and as the Prophet says: "The breach in the wall falleth suddenly when no man looketh for it." (*Is.* 30:13). The will, which was once united with God, and converted to God, has begun gradually to avert itself from God. There is no such thing as an equilibrium between God and sin; that cannot be; and when the will loses its union with God, it immediately inclines itself towards sin.

There is a thought which is indeed terrific, and ought to alarm every one of us who is conscious, as we are, of committing venial sins with such facility. St. Theresa said: "If I were to commit venial sin, I feel as if I should die; and that because every sin we commit, we commit in God." It is in God; for in Him we live, and move, and are; by Him we are sustained; our very being is supported by His being; the very power we abuse,

when we transgress His law, is power He has lent to us,
as the Prophet says, speaking for God: "You made Me
to serve with your sins, and wearied Me with your iniquities." That is, God is physically united with us, even
in the very actions we do against Him. We use the
powers of nature against the will of God in His grace.
Therefore it is that these venial sins, as they are called,
are in themselves great, as you will see hereafter; and
they dispose the soul towards greater sin for this
reason, that they keep up the trade of sinning, they
blunt the conscience, they bring on insensibility, they
cloud the sense of the presence of God, they familiarize
us with abusing the power which God has given us,
against Himself.

4. Then, fourthly, such sins displease God; and can
any sin be small which displeases God? When we walk
about at noonday, we walk about in the full splendor of
the noonday light—we are bathed in it, encompassed by
it—we cannot escape from it, go where we may—if we
go on the north side of a wall, the light is still there. So
it is with the presence of God. All our deeds, words,
and thoughts are in the presence of God: in the light of
the rays of the Divine holiness, justice, truth, mercy,
which inundate the soul as the light of the noonday in-
undates the world. Everything we do, we do before
Him, of whom St. John says: "His eyes are like a flame
of fire." (*Apoc.* 1:14). We displease God, then, as our
Father and as our Maker. We knowingly displease Him
by ungrateful and unfilial disobedience. It is as if the
Prodigal, after his return home and after being rein-
vested with the "first robe, and the ring on his hand,
shoes on his feet," and after receiving the "kiss of
peace," had again begun—and with his eyes open—to
murmur and complain at his father's will. We displease

also our Divine Redeemer, who died for us, our Divine Friend, and we displease Him by mean, treacherous, tricky, and hateful violations of the duties of friendship. And, thirdly, we displease and grieve the Holy Ghost; ay, we grieve the Holy Ghost by things which we think splendid, noble, laudable, admirable. I will give you some examples.

In society, a man is thought dull and stupid who cannot talk about his neighbor and satirically describe and make others laugh at his humorous descriptions of the failings and faults, and sometimes of the sins, of those that are known to him. A man that is simple in his conversation and bridles his tongue is a dull companion. He chills society. They are the most popular in society who have no bridle in their mouth, who will say anything, criticize anybody, ridicule all things, dress up and satirize every person, every event, and every scandal of the day. These are the entertaining men in society; these are the men that make their way. I should like to know, when they go home at night, how many sins of the tongue—venial sins, or perhaps mortal sins—have been written down in the book of God's remembrance; and I should like to know how many sins of listening to that detraction, and encouraging it by curiosity and laughter, have been written down also in the page of remembrance for those who heard it.

Take another example—those who go into the world, dressed out in the vanity and folly and ostentation of what is called "fashion." I wonder by what name it will be known in the Last Judgment. "Fashion" is a word in the mouths of men and women—have the holy angels got any equivalent word, and will "fashion" be written down in the book of God's remembrance? What will it be called? Vanity, willful tempting of others, vainglory,

luxury, self-exhibition; ay, and that often to the peril
and danger of those who look on.[3] You have seen what
looks like bloom upon the fruit. It is not bloom, but
blight. This blight upon the social characters of those
who please the world is thought to be a perfection; but
if you take a microscope, and if you look at that false
bloom, you will see that it is alive. It is a vile blight, it
is an animal disease, eating the fruit; and if the
microscope is powerful enough, and the light is clear
enough, you will see the miserable parasites moving in
all their repulsive reality.

What, I ask, are these venial sins of vanity, of pride,
of detraction, and others which I will not specify—what
are they? I will call them by their true name—the vermin of the human soul. They are the worms of death;
the worms that will feed on the body are but typical of
the vermin on the human soul; and in the light of God's
presence they are seen at this moment as the blight on
the fruit through the lens, and so they will be seen by us
in all their deformity in the light of the Day of Judgment.

5. Lastly, there is one other effect of venial sin, of
which I will speak. Just as a small ailment may become
a mortal sickness, so a venial sin may become a mortal
sin, and that with great facility. Not that any number of
venial sins, if they be heaped together, would make a
mortal sin; but they may put off their character and
stature of venial sins, and they may put on the
character and rise to the stature of deadly, or mortal,
sins. This they do in five ways.

First of all, a sin which is in itself venial may be
committed with the intention of covering or ac-
complishing some mortal sin, and then it is mortal too.
Or, secondly, it may be committed with a consciousness

that it will certainly lead to a mortal sin, and yet, nevertheless, it is persevered in. Or, thirdly, it may be done with a knowledge of God's prohibition, an open-eyed consciousness, and out of contempt of just authority. Or, fourthly, it may be so publicly and notoriously done as to give scandal to others, and to encourage and invite them to commit grave sin. Or, lastly, it may be done in the proximate peril of falling into mortal sin, and that with our eyes open; and thus to expose ourselves to mortal sin is mortal in itself.

Now, to give an example of what I mean. Suppose a man to tell a lie in a very light matter—some little deceit. He is asked, "Is such a one in this place?" He answers, "No," because he intends thereby to cover and to commit a mortal sin. The two sins then become one. Or, if I take a book—some book of levity, which may not in itself be positively wrong—and begin to read it on a Sunday morning, and I am determined I will finish it; and I know that in half an hour it is my duty to go to Holy Mass. I am bound under the strictest obedience, under mortal sin, to obey the precept of the Church, and nevertheless I go on reading, indulging myself, disregarding my duty, until at last I turn my back on our Divine Lord. Or, let me suppose that I am reading a book, and as I read on, I become conscious that the matter of it is contrary to the revelation or the holiness of God. Now, the world is full of books that are written against Christianity. There are the criticisms of rationalists, and the scoffs of false science. Do not misunderstand me. All true science comes from God. We have no fear of science in all its perfection; but there is a science, falsely so called, which is a stupidity. A science which is contrary to the revelation of God is not a science.

Suppose, then, I have a book in my hand, with some unbelieving criticisms, or rationalistic interpretations, or arguments against revelation, or some misapplications of science with false data, to prove that the world was not created, or is eternal, and the like. I come gradually upon this matter; and if I act upon my faith and conscience, I should put that book down. I know that whatever is contrary to the revelation of God may destroy my faith; but if I go on curiously reading it, without call of duty, with the light of God and His revelation shining in judgment on the page of the book, I am tempting God. And I will further suppose that standing by me are some who look up to me as an example, as children look up to their fathers and mothers, or younger brothers and sisters to their elder. They see me poring over that book, and I go on doing so in their sight; will they not do the same when I have left the room, and have I not set them the example, for the consequences of which I shall have to answer at the Day of Judgment?

Or, lastly, suppose I know perfectly well the book I am reading will turn up in two or three pages some abomination, such as are profusely written—not, I thank God, so much in this country as in a country not far off, and yet profusely imported into this. I grieve to know that on the tables in families and homes where the Name of God is honored, there lie books which ought to be burned, ay, and burned with the marks of public infamy; not burned simply that they may disappear in smoke, but that they may be gibbeted and condemned by the detestation of all pure-minded men and women. If I have one of those in my hand, and know if I read on I shall meet these abominations face to face—and yet continue to read—I am exposing myself to a danger of mortal sin. My mind may be stained by the abomination of that book; and, as a man that touches a leper may be infected, and may never be healed, if I make my mind leprous, the scales of that leprosy may never be cleansed away.

That which begins as a venial sin may easily end in mortal. There are two examples I would fain give if time would permit me. The one is theaters. I do not deny that theaters may be innocent—that to go to a theater may be lawful. I have been often asked during the long years of my duty in directing souls whether it is lawful to go to a theater. My answer has been always: If the representation is not bad in itself, I cannot forbid you. If you ask me what I advise, I say, without hesitation: Do not go. I cannot lay it upon you as a prohibition.

This, I know, will sound rigorous; nevertheless, it is the better choice; it is the more excellent way. I do not say it is the way of obligation. The Apostle says, "All things to me are lawful, but all things are not expedient" (*1 Cor.* 6:12); therefore I distinguish and say: Those things which are lawful I cannot forbid; but those things, though not forbidden, I counsel you with all my heart to renounce.

As to theaters, there may be, indeed, innocent representations; but I ask your own consciences, look over the representations which in a country, as I say, not far off, during this last winter, have been described to us by eye-witnesses. No man who has a pure heart, no man whose face is susceptible of the noblest and manliest suffusion, of a blush, could, if he remember himself, set his foot in any theater where such a representation is to be seen—I will not say no woman; I leave that to yourselves. As to our own theaters, I thank God it is not often they are openly and publicly stained.

Such things happen sometimes. Such scandals are imported among us: it is not only English dramas that are presented to us. I leave the whole of this to your own consciences, saying only that I would to God that those who can refrain from such things, as an offering to our Divine Redeemer, would refrain forever. When people say, "It does me no harm," I say to myself, "You do not know what harm it does you. You are not conscious how much has been taken off from the bloom of your mind, or from the clear purity of your eye and heart, by what you have seen, heard, and been conscious of, even though it has neither met the ear nor the eye."

One more example. If there is anything in the world which causes deterioration of character, manifold temptation, obscuration of mind, darkening and tainting of heart, it is dangerous friendships. The friends we choose—friends that are pleasant to us or flatter us, whose heart within, though known to God, is not suspected by men, and yet perhaps known to us—may be a world of temptation. Choose your friends from among the friends of God. Be not united with any that are separated from Him; for they will breathe into your ear, while you are unconscious, that which will pervade your whole spiritual being. All the dangerous temptations that you are likely to be exposed to—books, theaters, and the like—are as nothing compared to a dangerous friendship.

I will now simply sum up what I have said. The consequences of venial sins are, first of all, diminution of grace, the hindrance of the reception and operation of grace, the predisposing of the soul to mortal sin, the displeasing of God the Father, Son, and Holy Ghost, and the unspeakable facility with which those venial sins may pass into mortal.

In the commencement, I said I hoped to satisfy you before I finished, that venial sins are not small sins. Not many words are necessary. No sin can be small which is a great offense against a great God—against a great Majesty, a great Authority, a great Purity, a great Justice, a great Truth. No sins can be small which can only be cleansed away in the Precious Blood of the Incarnate Son of God. Yes; not the least venial sin that was ever committed can be absolved but through the Precious Blood which was shed upon the Cross. "Little sins!" God have mercy on those who talk this language! Once more. The least venial sin grieves the Holy Ghost. Can any sin be small which grieves the Spirit of God, of whom it is said, "All sin and blasphemy shall be forgiven unto men, save only the blasphemy against the Holy Ghost"?[1] Lastly, the venial sins we so easily commit will detain us from the vision of God after death, we know not how long. Though they do not, like mortal sin, separate us from the vision of God to all eternity, they will—we know not how long—separate us until every pain has been borne, and every sin has been expiated.

My last word, dear brethren, shall be very practical. Disorderly minds—that is, minds that live without rule, minds that have no order in their life—are always in danger of venial sins, and therefore of mortal—always walking on the brink of the precipice, always on the very verge, always putting their foot into the net. Now, I will give you one easy rule of practice. Every day of your life place yourselves, as I have said, under that noonday sun of God's perfections, and pray to God the Holy Ghost to illuminate your hearts with such a knowledge of God and of yourselves, that, in the light of His perfection, you may see the least deviation of your thoughts, words, and deeds from His holy will.

There was a time when you—every one of you—were white as snow; in your baptismal innocence you were spotless, you had not then a stain! The Precious Blood had cleansed away Original Sin, and as yet you had not contracted mortal sin, and perhaps in your childhood few venial sins. In the sight of the Judge, in the sight of your Redeemer, what are you now! What spots, what stains dark as night and red as scarlet! How is all that beauty and whiteness destroyed by ill habits, not of mortal sin—remember, I am not speaking of that now—but by venial sins of tempers, jealousies, envy, sloth, neglect of God, self-indulgence! The examples I have given are sufficient—sins of the tongue, sins of personal ostentation, sins of reading, sins of worldly pleasure, sins of dangerous friendship.

What are you now? Where is the white robe of your Baptism? And as to the debt of pain for sins, unless a life of penance, self-denial, generous sorrow shall cleanse away those debts in this life, there remains but one way, the fires of Purgatory, in which those sins can be expiated. Hear the Word of God: "Other foundation can no man lay than that which is laid; which is Jesus Christ. Now if any man build upon this foundation gold, silver, precious stones, wood, hay, stubble, every man's work shall be made manifest; for the day shall declare it, because it shall be revealed by fire; and the fire shall try every man's work of what sort it is. If any man's work abide which he hath built thereupon, he shall receive a reward. If any man's work burn, he shall suffer loss [therefore those words are spoken not of mortal sinners, those words are altogether spoken of those who have upon them only venial sins]: but he himself shall be saved, yet so as by fire." (*1 Cor.* 3:11-15).

NOTES

1. The sin referred to in this Bible passage (*Matt.* 12:31) is that blasphemy by which the Pharisees attributed the miracles of Christ, wrought by the Holy Ghost, to Beelzebub, the prince of devils. Now this kind of sin is usually accompanied by so much obstinacy and such willful opposing of the Spirit of God and the known truth that men who are guilty of it are seldom or never converted: and therefore they are never forgiven because they will not repent. Otherwise there is no sin which God cannot or will not forgive to such as sincerely repent and have recourse to the keys of the Church. See also p. 16, p. 24 and p. 107.
2. See p. 125 for further explanation of this Bible passage and of the difference between sin and concupiscence.
3. Sins of immodest fashions may be mortal, depending on the degree of immodesty and the wearer's intention.

Sermon IV

SINS OF OMISSION

"Who can understand sins? From my secret sins cleanse me, O God."

—Psalm 18:13

If, as we have seen, the knowledge of the intellect and the consent of the will be necessary to constitute a sin, how can there be secret sins—how can there be sins which we do not know? First, because we may have committed what we have afterwards forgotten, which thus becomes secret to us, but is yet recorded in the book of God's remembrance. Next, we may only half understand the sinfulness of that which we do, and one-half of our guilt is secret from us. Again, through a culpable ignorance of ourselves, we do not know how often we offend God. We read in Holy Scripture these words, which at first sight are most alarming: "There are wise men, and there are just men, and their work is in the hand of God; yet no man knoweth whether he be worthy of love or hatred." (*Eccles.* 9:1). That is, even the just man, even the wise man, even the man that does many works which are remembered before God, even he cannot know with a perfect consciousness whether in the sight of God he be an object of love or an object of hatred,[1] that is, whether or not he be in the state of grace; and that because in the light of the presence of God sins which are perfectly invisible to us, sins of thought, word, and deed—which, in the twilight of our conscience, in the confusion of our soul, are secret to us—are visible to God.

They who know this best can only have here the confidence of hope that their sins before God are forgiven. They have no revelation of it, and therefore they cannot know it with a Divine certainty; and that which we do not know with a Divine certainty, we can only know by a trust of confidence and hope springing from the promises of God, and the consciousness of our own soul.[2] This must be manifest to everyone who at all knows himself. He knows that the leaves which fall from the trees in autumn are not more in multitude than the words we scatter every day; that the lights of the sun, glancing to and fro all the day long, are not more multitudinous than the thoughts perpetually rising in our hearts; that the motion of the sea, or the restlessness of the air, is not more continuous than the working of our imagination, our heart, our affections, our passions; and in this mystery, this confusion of our being, who is there that will venture to say that the good predominates over the evil, the light over the darkness, and that in the sight of God he is an object of love rather than of hatred?

Now I have felt that our subjects hitherto have been of a severe kind, and the subject that we have now will not be less so; but hereafter I hope we shall be able to pass on to the grace and the mercy of our Lord Jesus Christ, and to the consolations for which all that I have said is but the preparation. We are approaching to our Easter joys; that is, to the Precious Blood of Jesus Christ and to the perfect absolution of sin, which He has laid up for all those who are penitent. Let me, then, take up and complete this last part of what I have said.

We have already seen the nature of sins of commission. They are either the mortal sins, which separate the soul from God in this life, and, if not repented of, in the life to come; or they are the venial sins, which are the disease though they are not the death of the soul; and these are the greatest evils, next after mortal sin, that the heart of man can conceive. They are the preludes of mortal sin in many, and are punished by detention from the vision of God, both in this world and in the world to come. This, then, was the first part of our subject; the last part will be sins of omission. The first was the sin of doing evil; the last, the sin of leaving good undone.

Now let me suppose that which is intellectually conceivable, though it has never existed; let me suppose a soul created in the likeness of God, and committing no sin, but bearing no fruit. This is precisely the state described in the parable of the barren fig tree. The tree was alive, the root strong and in the ground, the branches were covered with leaves—but when, year after year, the fruit was sought, none was to be found. This is a parable and description of a soul, alive indeed, but not fulfilling the end of its creation. And for what end was the soul created? To know, to love, to serve, to worship, and to be made like to God; and a soul that does not fulfill the end of its creation, that does not know and love and serve and worship God, and is not likened and assimilated to God its Maker and its Original—that soul, not fulfilling the end of its creation, would therefore be in a state of condemnation, and the words of the parable would be true and just: "Cut it down. Why cumbereth it the ground?" (*Luke* 13:7).

We are bound by three obligations to glorify God by

fulfilling the end of our creation. First, by the law of our creation itself. We were created to glorify Him by a life of obedience as much as the earth was created to bear fruit, and the firmament to give light. If the firmament were turned into darkness, and the earth into desolation, they would not fulfill the end for which they were made; and so, too, with the soul that does not glorify God. Again, we are bound to glorify God by a direct commandment, and that direct commandment is written in the Decalogue and in the two precepts of charity: "Thou shalt love the Lord thy God with thy whole heart, with thy whole soul, with thy whole mind, with thy whole strength, and thy neighbor as thyself." (*Matt.* 22:37, 39). And we are bound to fulfill these two precepts of charity under pain of eternal death.

There is also a third obligation—not indeed binding under pain of eternal death, a law of which I shall speak hereafter—and that is the law of liberty: the law of love, of gratitude, and of generous freedom, which is written by the Holy Ghost on the heart of all those who, being born again in Baptism, are united to our Lord and Saviour Jesus Christ by the bond of Charity.

Sins of omission are against either the law of our creation, or the law of the two precepts of charity, or against the law of liberty. If we leave undone the good or the duties to which we are bound by those obligations, we commit sins of omission. Sins of omission may be mortal, but we shall begin by considering venial sins of omission. I have already shown how sins that are venial lead to sins that are mortal, so I will now show how sins of omission, in addition to being sins in themselves, also lead on to sins of commission. They are the beaten pathway which leads to sins of commission.

Now a sin of omission, or the leaving of duty undone,

may indeed arise from any one of the seven capital sins, and then it is also a sin of commission. A son may omit his duty to his father through anger. The sin of anger adds a sin of commission. So I might take examples from the others; but I will select one only, and that because it has the greatest affinity to sins of omission; I mean the sin of sloth.

We understand at once that pride, anger, jealousy, and the like may be mortal sins, because we can understand their intrinsic hatefulness and guilt; but sometimes men say, "How can a sin of sloth be mortal?" We must therefore distinguish. The sin of slothfulness is not mortal except under certain circumstances; but a state of sloth and a habit of sloth is certainly a mortal sin. We must therefore distinguish between slothfulness and sloth. Slothfulness is the habit or state of the soul, tending towards the last mortal state of sloth, which I will describe hereafter. Let us take this as our example, and I will show how this slothfulness leads to sins of omission, and how these sins of omission lead to sins of commission, and how these sins of commission at last terminate in the mortal sin of sloth.

1. Suppose, then, some Christian, who is in the state of grace and communion with God, living in Charity, in the love of God and the love of his neighbor—that is, leading a good and pious life. One of the chief duties which he will punctually and carefully fulfill is the duty of prayer. You will remember in the Book of Acts, when Saul the persecutor was converted by a special miracle, the sign given of his conversion was this: "Behold he prayeth." (*Acts* 9:11). Prayer is the breath of the soul. Just as breathing is the sign of life, prayer is the sign of the life of the soul. Prayer means the union of the soul with God, the converse of the soul with

God, the soul speaking with God, "ascending to God," as St. Augustine says, "by thought," that is, in meditation; "by the affections," that is, in worship; and "by the will," that is, making resolutions of obedience. Every day, a man who is a Christian and living in a state of grace will pray to Almighty God, not only morning and night, but at other times in the day. Prayer will be his habit.

Now, what is the effect of sins of omission in respect to prayer? Let me suppose that business, professions, pleasure, worldly distractions, begin to break the habit of prayer. Perhaps at first a man only shortens his prayers; or he does not even shorten them, he says them more hastily. He says them materially as before, but not mentally, for his heart is somewhere else. He is in haste, and though he repeats literally his usual prayers, his heart is far off: or, at least, he ceases to pray with the same sweetness and goodwill and fixedness and recollection.

Here is an example of a sin of omission which is very common. I do not take the example of a man giving up his prayers—that stands to reason—but even if he begins to omit the fervor and recollection with which he says his prayers, what does it lead on to? A certain wandering of the mind, a multiplicity of thoughts which crowd upon him—the associations, which glance off, as it were, from every angle of his memory and of his intellect. His mind is full of colors cast in from the world, even while kneeling before God. Little by little his mind gets the habit of wandering, and then he begins to complain that he cannot pray. When he kneels down, his heart is in his house of business, or in the pleasures of last night, or in the amusements of tomorrow. He is, as we say, in the state of distraction or of dissipation;

his mind is scattered, he has lost his recollection.

What is the next step? He begins to talk much, to scatter his words without consideration. A man of prayer has a habit of weighing, of measuring his words. As he has the habit of prayer, so he will have the habit of silence; he will be what we call an interior man. His mind will be turned in on itself. He will not be a chatterer; but men who begin to lose their habit of recollection before God become chatterers among men. Solitude becomes irksome; to be alone is torment; to be silent is a pain—he must be always speaking. An uneasiness of being alone with themselves makes such men seek for society; and a desire to get rid of uneasy recollections makes them continually talk: and in this way they commit a multitude of faults by their tongue. But for every idle word that men shall speak, they shall account in the Day of Judgment. (*Matt.* 12:36).

Well, there is worse than this. St. Paul of the Cross used to say to those about him, "Stay at home; stay at home." When they asked, "What do you mean? Am I never to go out of my house?" he would answer them, "Stay in the solitude of your own heart before God, and keep three lamps always burning before the altar— Faith, Hope, and Charity—before the presence of God in your heart." Now, the man I have been describing began, perhaps, with thoughtfulness; but little by little the dissipation of his thoughts and the constant talk of his lips have made him to be, as we say, "all aboard." He is not "at home"; he is not dwelling with God; the three lamps grow dim; Faith, Hope and Charity burn low. This is just the state that our Divine Lord has described when He says: "Any man putting his hand to the plough and looking back, is not fit for the kingdom of God." (*Luke* 9:62). He does not say that he will never be saved, because he may turn back and steadily follow out the furrow to the end; but so long as he has his face averted from God, all the activity of his mind and being is turned from God to creatures.

2. This is the first effect of a sin of omission; the next is that it produces a kind of sluggishness in everything that he does. Outwardly, perhaps, the actions of his life are to the eye of his neighbors just the same as they were before; but to the eye of God, a change has passed upon him. The eye of God, to whom all things are open, sees that the inward state of that man is not what it was. There is a certain sluggishness which no human eye can detect, but God sees it in everything that he does. I have said before, that fervor consists in doing our duty with great exactness. He begins to do his duties with a certain carelessness, so that the motives from which he acts, and the manner in which he does even things that are good, are not what they were. Just as a man who writes in haste, or who draws in haste, will not complete any figure or any letter with exactness; so it is with the man who begins to lose his fervor.

Then he begins to be unpunctual. He puts off his prayers in the morning; he forgets them till noonday, and perhaps, at noonday, he says only half of them; and at night he says them with an uneasy conscience. Perhaps the next day it is the same, or even worse. Unpunctuality begins to run through all his secret duties before God. Then comes irregularity. That is to say, he used to live by rule, he used to take the will of God as his will, and try to conform himself to it as well as he could; but now he lives by the rules of the world, the customs of men, and I may say, at haphazard and at random.

The next step is this: he begins openly to leave duties

undone. To take one example: everyone who is in a
state of grace has the seven gifts of the Holy Ghost.
Now these seven gifts are: Wisdom, Understanding,
Counsel, Knowledge, Piety, Fortitude, and the Fear of
the Lord. Four of these perfect the intellect, and three
of them perfect the will; but a man in this state of sluggishness ceases to act according to the light and direction of these gifts of the Holy Spirit of God. These
seven gifts have been described as the sails of a ship;
the more we spread them the more we speed the soul;
and the more we speed the soul the more we are carried
onwards in the way of salvation. Those who neglect
those gifts, who do not make use of them, leave the
sails reefed or furled; and their course in the way of
eternal life is retarded.

Again, there are in every one of us who is in the state
of grace, the virtues of Faith, Hope, and Charity. In
your prayerbooks you are bid to make the acts of these
three virtues. But what do acts mean? They are inward
actions of the soul towards God, whereby we exert the
grace of Faith, or the grace of Hope, or the grace of
Charity in union with God. But these soon lose their
power in a man who has ceased to pray. Next comes
neglect of the manifold duties of Charity towards our
neighbor. What was the sin of the Priest and of the
Levite when each of them saw the wounded man in the
road between Jerusalem and Jericho? The Priest came
that way, and looked upon him, and passed by. The
Levite came, and saw him, and passed on. They committed a sin of omission, in respect to the charity they
owed to their neighbor. What was the sin of Dives, at
whose door Lazarus lay full of sores? We do not read
that he refused to help him—we certainly do not read
that he drove him away from his house—but he gave

him no help. It was a sin of omission. Our Lord says
that at the Last Day He will say: "I was hungry, and ye
gave me no meat; I was thirsty, and ye gave me no
drink; I was naked, and ye clothed me not." (*Matt.*
25:35). He will not say: "I asked you, and you refused
Me"; but "Ye did not seek Me out," which again is a
sin of omission.

Lastly comes the sin of omission of love towards
God. We are bound to love God with our whole heart
and our whole mind; and the man who commits sins of
omission in Charity towards his neighbor fails also in
Charity towards God, for "he that loveth not his
brother whom he seeth, how can he love God whom he
seeth not?" (*1 John* 4:20). The state of such a soul is
thus described in the parable: the servant who had
received a pound took and buried it, and another who
had received a talent wrapped it in a napkin. When the
Lord came they both restored that which they had
received, undiminished; but it was not increased—and
why? Because they were guilty of a sin of omission.
They had not used that trust which was committed to
their stewardship; and the excuse given was this: "I
knew that thou wert an austere man, reaping where
thou hast not sown, and gathering where thou hast not
strewed." (*Luke* 19:21). That is to say, when he had
begun to lose his love to his Master, he lost his confidence in his Master's love. He began to distrust the love
of God, because he knew that he was wanting in love
towards Him. So that the sin of omission at last
threatens the life of the soul: for Charity is the life of
the soul.

3. Then, thirdly, from these sins comes a certain
animosity against those who love God. Just as the soul
turns away from God, in that proportion it has an

animosity against those who continue to persevere in
the love of God; so much so, that the very sight of anyone who is fervent in the love of God becomes an
eyesore. We know—and you, I have no doubt, know by
your own experience—that we can tolerate anybody as
a companion who is less pious than we are, but we cannot easily tolerate anybody who is more pious. Anyone
who prays more, or anyone who makes more of his
duties towards God and his neighbor—anyone who is
more just or more holy—is a constant reproof and
rebuke to us. We are ill at ease in his presence, but
anybody who is lower than ourselves we can tolerate
easily. He is neither a reproof nor a rebuke; on the contrary, we think we can teach him, and we are soothed
by thinking that we can set him an example. There is
nothing galling or painful in the companionship of
those who are lower than ourselves in the spiritual life;
but those who are above us, unless we are humble,
make us restless.

One sign of those who are declining from God is this:
they do not like to see people go so often to Communion; they get impatient at hearing of their going so
often to confession; or if they know that they often visit
the Blessed Sacrament, or that they spend a long time
in their room in prayer—all this makes them uneasy.
Finally, even the grace of God which they see in others
becomes to them a trial. If they see people more
zealous than they are, more fervent, more self-denying,
more prosperous in working for God—in saving souls,
in doing works of charity, or in labors of spiritual mercy—even that very spiritual prosperity of their neighbor
makes them to fret. They are conscious that they are
not like them, and that consciousness is painful.

If you look for an example out of Holy Scripture, I

will give you two. When the Prodigal Son came home and the father forgave him, and gave him shoes on his feet, and the first robe, and made the festival of joy— the elder brother, when he heard the music, refused to come in. He was jealous and angry. (*Luke* 15:22). When our Divine Lord sat in the house of Simon the Pharisee—and poor Mary Magdalen, with all her sins upon her, burst into the midst of that banquet and washed the feet of our Lord with her tears and anointed them and kissed them, Simon the Pharisee said to himself: "This man, if he were a prophet, would know who and what manner of woman this is, for she is a sinner." Our Lord said: "Simon, I have somewhat to say to thee. I entered into thy house; thou gavest me no water for my feet: this woman since I came in hath washed my feet with her tears. My head with oil thou didst not anoint; but she hath anointed my feet with ointment. Thou gavest me no kiss; she, since I came in, kissed my feet." (*Luke* 7:40, 44-46). In the heart of that Pharisee, upright as no doubt he was, and pure from the sins which stained poor Mary Magdalen, there was a lack of charity before God, a pride and censoriousness, which was rebuked by the grace of penance in that poor fallen woman.

4. A fourth effect of the sins of omission and of this decline of the soul is despondency, which is akin to despair. A consciousness of sin has the effect of depressing the soul, and, unless it soften it, of making it to doubt its own salvation; for where the Charity of God and our neighbor has become low and faint, if it be not altogether lost, there both Hope and Faith begin likewise to decline. Any man who is conscious of his own sins knows that though men do not see them or suspect them—and though they are only half known

and half seen even by his own conscience—they are all
perfectly seen and known to the eye of Almighty God.

This consciousness of sinfulness, coupled with the
consciousness of impenitence, the sense that he is not
softened, nor humbled, but rather that he is irritated by
the clear sight of his own sin and of the graces of those
that are about him, lights up a high fever of resentful
heat which grows more fierce as Charity declines. The
will in its stiffness refuses to bow itself before God, and
though a cloud on the conscience half hides many sins
that are not altogether forgotten, he is half conscious of
many, and therefore full of fear, not knowing whether
or no he is the object of a final hatred. A soul in that
state becomes desponding and reckless, so that in a
multitude of cases, instead of turning towards God by
repentance, it turns recklessly away from God and
plunges further into sin.

So long as there is a hope of salvation, a hope of pardon, and so long as a good name and fame among men
is not lost, a man is sustained by a certain lingering
confidence and restrained from a multitude of sins; but
the moment hope is lost and the last spring is broken, a
man who began only with sins of omission and then sins
of sloth, will at last plunge recklessly into sins he never
committed before, saying: "It is too late—I have gone
too far—I am too bad. Spots are not visible upon a
black garment, and I am black before God, whether I
am so before man or not"; on this, he plunges himself
further and further into sin. Those who answer to this
description verify the words of our Divine Lord to the
church of Sardis: "I know thy works, and that thou hast
the name of being alive, and thou art dead. Be watchful
and strengthen the things that remain which are ready
to die. For I find not thy works full before my God."

(*Apoc.* 3:1-2). The meaning of this is: Thou hast lost thy first Charity; there remain Faith and Hope in a little measure. The reed, though bruised, is not broken—the flax, though smoking only, is not quenched; there is Hope yet, for Faith and Hope are not yet dead; but when once Hope is dead, what can remain?

Take example from Scripture. Judas sold his Master; Peter denied Him. Judas lost his hope, but Peter hoped yet; and Peter went out and wept bitterly, and was forgiven; and Judas went out and hanged himself.

5. Lastly, there is one more effect, and that is the state which is the mortal sin of sloth—the state of the soul which, having fallen from Charity and having lost Hope, has become sick of God and weary of God. Such a man may even say: "I wish to God that I had never been born!" I have heard those words again and again out of the mouth of sinners: "I wish to God I had never heard the name of Jesus Christ; I should not then have been responsible. I would to God I had never known the truth; for I should not have to answer for it. I should die like a dog—and better to die like a dog than die as I shall, with the illumination to know God and Jesus Christ, to know His will, and His truth, and to be forever as I am now!" Such things every priest has heard, and perhaps you yourselves have heard. The soul, weary and sick of God, turns away from the Holy Sacraments, turns away from prayer, turns away from holy people, from every memorial of God and His service, until at last such a man will say: "Almighty God, why dost Thou persecute me with Thy perfections? Thy justice, which I cannot deny, is like the blaze of the noonday sun, terrible and scorching; and Thy holiness is like the light that pervades the world, and I cannot escape from it." Souls in that state say in an inverted

sense the very words of the Psalmist: "Whither shall I go from thy presence, and whither shall I flee from thy face? If I go up in heaven, thou art there; if I go down into hell, thou art there also. If in the morning I take wings and flee to the uttermost parts of the earth, even there thy hand leadeth me, and thy right hand upholdeth me. If I say, Darkness shall cover me, the darkness is no darkness to thee. The darkness and the light to thee are both alike." (*Ps.* 138:7-12).

This is what the people of Jerusalem said: the forefathers of those who cried, "His blood be upon us and upon our children." (*Matt.* 27:25). They said: "Let the Holy One of Israel cease from before us" (*Is.* 30:11); that is, let God get out of our way. Now, brethren, this is what the sin of sloth comes to at last. I have traced it from its beginning in a sin of omission—a sin of omission in prayer; because, as I said, prayer is the life and breath of the soul, and the soul that prays is united with God. The soul that loses its union with God by prayer may fall into the bottomless pit. There is no depth of eternal death into which a soul that ceases to pray may not fall. It will not fall all at once; it falls very gradually, little by little, insensibly, and there is the chief danger. This exactly expresses the words with which I began: "Who can understand sins? From my secret sins cleanse me, O Lord."

I hope, then, that I need speak no more upon this severe part of our subject. I will only give two very short counsels. The one is this: aim at the highest and greatest things of God's kingdom. Do not think that it is humility to try to live a commonplace Christian life. Dear brethren, it is like seamen who say, "I will not launch out into the deep, but I will keep near the shore." To keep near the shore is not always safety; to keep near the shore requires the greater seamanship; to keep near the shore may be to run the greatest risk of wrecking. Do not imagine for one moment that this is humility. The humblest may seek the greatest things in God's kingdom. Aim at the highest. You have been called to be saints, every one of you. The very name by which we are called in the New Testament is "saints." With all your sins and imperfections about you, you are called to be saints. If you are to be saved, saints you must be before the throne in the kingdom of God hereafter. Saints you are now, if the Holy Ghost dwell in you, and you are united in love (that is, in that supernatural Charity which accompanies sanctifying grace) to God and your neighbor. Sanctity is in you; and as the twilight of the morning is the light of the day, and differs from the noonday only in the degree of its splendor, so the sanctity which is in you now differs only in the degree of its manifestation from that perfect sanctity which shall be in you when "the just shall shine as the sun in the kingdom of their Father." (*Matt.* 13:43). Is it possible, then, that we can aim at anything lower than this?

It is a deceit of the devil for any man to turn aside, under the notion of humility or of impossibility, from the path which leads him upward to the highest Christian life. The grace that is given to each one of you is measured according to the vocation wherewith you are called. If God has called you to be saints, He has given you, and will give you, grace sufficient to enable you to become saints—ay, the guiltiest among you, and there may be some ears listening to my words conscious of the stain of mortal sin. Even the guiltiest that hears me has grace offered now, at this moment, to become penitent, and through penitence to become a saint. The most tempted, the most buffeted, the soul that has fallen oftenest, that has been cast down over and over again by long habitual and inveterate sin, even to that soul grace sufficient is offered at this time to be a saint if it have the will to receive it. More than this: the most slothful, the most sluggish souls, the souls most conscious that they are covered with sins of omission, and that there is not a duty they do which they do not do so tardily and imperfectly as to be utterly ashamed in secret of themselves before God, even such souls as these have the grace of fervor and zeal and strength and piety and perseverance offered at this moment if they have only the will to accept it. The only condition is this: break with the world, with sin, and with yourselves, and be on God's side. Take up your cross boldly; follow Jesus Christ. Have no compromises, no reserves, and He will do the rest for you.

The other counsel is this. Cast yourselves with all your offenses of commission and omission, all your faults, all your stains, all your weight, with the whole burden of your sins on you—cast yourselves upon the Sacred Heart of Jesus, as John lay upon His bosom at supper. Do not think that this is not for you. Do not say, "It is not for me to cast myself there where the beloved disciple lay." Why did he lie there? Was it because he loved his Lord? No; it was because his Lord loved him; and that same love which He had for John, not in degree it may be, but in kind, in its infinite tenderness and its infinite compassion, that same love is yours. He loves you, if not in the same measure, in the same manner, and therefore cast yourselves upon the love of our Lord.

The gift of free will, which we all have, is a perilous gift. It is a wonderful mystery that a man can balance and poise his body to stand or walk—every motion rests in a mysterious manner on the balance of nature; but the freedom of the will is still more mysterious, and still more easily cast down. We are surrounded by temptation all the day long, and the world is constantly playing upon us by its powers of assimilation. Worse than this, there is the treachery of false and subtle hearts, of hearts always ready to take fire. All the day long sin springs up within to meet the temptation from without. For that reason you have more need. Do not say, "That makes me less able to cast myself upon the Sacred Heart of my Redeemer." It is for that very reason that you need to do it. As the blind man went to the Pool of Siloe; as the lepers came within reach of the hand of our Saviour; as the poor woman touched the hem of His garment—so, as your miseries are the greater, you have the more need; and if you will come to Him, He, by His Spirit within you, and by His protection about you, will keep you from all evil, and will confirm you in His grace. And that you may do this, I will bid you adopt from this day one practice.

Every day of your life pray God to give you light to see yourselves just as He sees you now: to show you what sin is in all its hideousness, in all its subtilty, and to show you those secret sins which now you do not see in yourselves. Every day of your life ask this of God. Remember the young man who came to our Lord, and asked what he should do to inherit the kingdom of Heaven. Our Lord said: "Sell all thou hast and give to the poor, and come and follow me." (*Matt.* 19:21). He went away sorrowing, and that one thing wanting lost him all things.[3] You remember the five wise and the five foolish virgins. The five foolish virgins went out with the five that were wise; they were attired in the same bridal raiment; they all carried their lamps with them, and their lamps were lighted—in this they were all alike; and they all slumbered and slept. What was the difference between the five wise and the five foolish? The five wise had oil in their vessels with their lamps; the five foolish had omitted to bring oil in their vessels with their lamps. And while they all slumbered their lamps went out; and when the cry was heard at midnight, "The bridegroom cometh!" they waked up and found their lamps gone out. The five foolish virgins first would borrow; but it is impossible to borrow grace. They went to buy; but while they were gone the bridegroom entered, and the door was shut. When they came back they knocked upon the door, and said: "Lord, Lord, open to us." But He answered from within: "I never knew you."

NOTES

1. Because of God's absolute holiness, He has the hatred of abomination toward sin, though He does not have a hatred of enmity towards the person of the sinner.

2. The Council of Trent declared: "If one considers his own weakness and his defective disposition, he may well be fearful and anxious as to his state of grace, as nobody knows with the certainty of faith, which permits of no error, that he has achieved the grace of God." (This doctrine is in notable contrast to the Protestant doctrine that the justified possess the certainty of faith, which excludes all doubt, about their justification.) Sacred Scripture bears witness to the uncertainty of the state of justification (the state of grace); St. Paul said: "Neither do I judge my own self. For I am not conscious to myself of any thing, yet am I not hereby justified; but he that judgeth me, is the Lord." (*1 Cor.* 4:3-4). Also: "With fear

and trembling work out your salvation." (*Phil.* 2:12). The reason for the uncertainty of the state of grace lies in this, that without a special revelation nobody can with the certainty of faith know whether or not he has fulfilled all the conditions which are necessary for the achieving of justification [e.g., whether his contrition was sincere and entire]. However, the impossibility of the certainty of faith by no means excludes a high moral certainty supported by the testimony of conscience. Cf. *Summa Theologica* Ia IIae, 112, 5. This lack of infallible assurance must not be made a matter for scrupulous worry. Also, it should be noted that Catholics habitually end the sacramental confession of their sins with the words, "For these and all the sins of my past life I am heartily sorry," thus expressing sorrow even for sins which may have been forgotten.

3. This young man did not necessarily lose his *soul* because he declined to follow a religious vocation—though such a refusal would indeed be spiritually dangerous, if religious life is the route to salvation which God has chosen for a particular soul.

Sermon V

THE GRACE AND THE SACRAMENT OF PENANCE

"Receive ye the Holy Ghost. Whose sins you shall forgive they are forgiven them; whose sins you shall retain, they are retained."

—John 20:22-23

It was late in the evening of the first day of the week when Jesus rose from the dead that His disciples were gathered together, and the doors were shut for fear of the Jews. When they least expected it, unawares, and by His divine power, He came—though the doors were closed—and stood in the midst of them; and His first words were, "Peace be unto you." And when He had assured them that it was He Himself, their fears were dispelled. He then said, "Receive ye the Holy Ghost. Tne Holy Ghost proceeds from the Father and from the Son, and I, the Son of God, breathe upon you—receive ye the Holy Ghost; whose sins you shall forgive, they are forgiven them; whose sins you shall retain, they are retained." That is, He gave them the proof of His Godhead in the power of absolution. He gave them the proof of His Godhead—for the Pharisees were right when they asked, "Who shall forgive sins but God only?" (*Mark* 2:7).

God alone can absolve, and God alone can give the power of absolution. When the power of absolution is exercised by any man, he is but an instrument in the hand of God: the absolver is always God Himself. Our Lord exercised, among many other attributes of His Godhead upon earth, these three special powers of divinity: He raised the dead; He multiplied the bread in the wilderness; and He cleansed the lepers—and these three works of almighty power, which are altogether divine, He has committed in a spiritual form to His Church forever. When He said, "Go, and make disciples of all nations, baptizing them in the name of the Father, Son, and Holy Ghost," in that power of Baptism He gave to His Apostles and their successors the power of raising from spiritual death to spiritual life. Those who are born dead in sin are raised by a new birth to spiritual life. When He instituted the most Holy Sacrament of His Body and Blood, and gave to His Church the authority to say, "This is My Body," He gave the power to feed His people with the Bread of Life, and to multiply that Bread forever. When He said, "Whose sins ye shall forgive, they are forgiven unto them," He gave the power of cleansing the leprosy of the soul.

Sometimes, incoherent—or, what is worse, controversial—minds imagine, or at least say, that this power was confined to the Apostles. The very words are enough to prove the contrary; but there is an intrinsic reason in the thing which, to any Christian mind, must be sufficient to show that these three powers are perpetual; for what are these three powers, but the authority to apply to the souls of men forever the benefits of the most Precious Blood of Jesus Christ? The Precious Blood would have been shed in vain, if it were not applied to the souls of men one by one. The most potent medicines work no cures, save in those to whom they are applied;

and the Precious Blood, which is the remedy of sin, works the healing of the soul only by its application. Baptism, the Holy Sacrament of the Altar, and the Sacrament of Penance are three divine channels whereby the Precious Blood of Jesus Christ is applied to the soul.

I am conscious that our thoughts hitherto have been full of sharpness and severity. We have been dwelling upon sin—upon mortal and venial sins, and upon sins of omission. We enter now upon another region—the realm of peace, of grace, of pardon and healing. Therefore we will speak of the grace and the works of penance.

Penance is both a virtue and a Sacrament. From the beginning of the world the grace of penance has been poured out upon men. It is an interior disposition of the soul before God; and from the beginning of the world the Holy Ghost, whose office it is to convince the world of sin, has convinced sinners of their transgressions, has converted them to penance, and from penance has made them saints. But penance, in the Christian law, is also a Sacrament; and I have to explain the meaning of the grace and the action of the Sacrament, and how they are united.

1. First, penance is a grace or inward disposition of the soul, and I need not go far to find an explanation. I need not frame any explanation of my own, for we have a divine delineation of what penance is, drawn, as it were, by a pencil of light by our Divine Saviour Himself in the parable of the Prodigal Son. There we have a revelation of what the grace of penance is.

You remember the parable. A man had two sons, and the younger came to him and said: "Give me the portion that falleth to me"; and when he had received it, he went into a far country and wasted it in riot, fell into misery and returned to his father, and was pardoned.

Let us take the main features of this. First, the son who, under the roof of a loving father, had need of nothing—for his father was rich—chafed and was fretful because the authority of a superior will was upon him. He could not bear the yoke of living under a paternal rule, and his imagination was all on fire with the thought of liberty. He looked at the horizon—it may be the mountains that bounded the lands and fields of his father—and pictured to himself the valleys and plains and cities full of youth and happiness and life and freedom—a happy land, if only he could break away from the restraints of home. He came to his father, and with a cold-hearted insolence said: "Give me the portion that falleth to me"; which being translated, is, "Give me what I shall have when you are dead." There was a spirit of undutifulness and of ingratitude in that demand—but the father gave it; and the parable says that not many days after—that is, with all speed, in fact—"gathering all things together," all he had and all he could get, he went off into a far country, and there he spent all he had in living riotously.

Then there came a mighty famine, and he, having spent all things, was reduced to beggary. His fair-weather friends all forsook him; the parasites who fed at his table all abandoned him: and those that spoke him fair when he was rich and had anything to give them, turned their backs upon him: his very servants were not to be seen. He found himself isolated, destitute, and brought to such extremity that "he went to one of the citizens of that country," and offered himself as his servant. The citizen accepted him; not into his house—he did not even send him into his garden, no, nor into his vineyard. He sent him into his fields; and not to tend his sheep, no, nor to watch over his oxen, but "to feed his swine." Such is the degradation of a sinner.

In that extremity of need no man gave to him; all his old friends were afar off; if they possessed anything, they kept it to themselves, or at least they gave nothing to him. There was no memory, no gratitude of their past friendship. He was fain to fill his hunger with the husks—not only the husks which the swine did eat, but the husks which the swine had left—the husks which fell, as it were, from the trough of a herd of swine. Reduced to such misery, which is the picture of a soul in mortal sin, as I have described before, he came to himself—the word is, he "returned to himself." He not only had left his father, but had forsaken himself—he was out of himself, beside himself; for sin is madness. When he returned to himself, he said: "How many hired servants of my father have bread in abundance, and I here perish for hunger. I will arise and go to my father, and will say unto him: Father, I have sinned against Heaven and before thee, and am no more worthy to be called thy son; make me as one of thy hired servants."

Here was the consciousness of unworthiness. He did not aspire to be a son again; that, he thought, was lost forever. It was enough for him, and he was content, to accept the position of a hired servant under his father's roof. And he arose and went to his father. And as he was coming—it may be, down the path of the mountainside, barefoot and ragged, up which he had gone a little while ago in all the bravery of his apparel and his pride—before he caught sight of his father, his father saw him afar off, for love gives keenness of sight to a father's eye: he saw his son returning, and he ran towards him. He was as eager to forgive as the son was to be forgiven—ay, more; he fell upon his neck, and the Prodigal Son began his confession: "Father, I have sinned against Heaven and before thee"; but before he could finish—the words "make me as one of thy hired servants" never came out of his mouth—his father fell upon his neck and kissed him, and forgave him all. He was perfectly absolved. And the father said: "Bring forth quickly"—that is, make haste, no delay—"the first robe," the robe he had before, and put it on him. Put shoes on his feet and a ring on his hand. Restore him not only to the state of pardon, but to the full possession of all he had before his fall; for this my son was dead, and is alive again; he was lost, and is found.

We see here in the Prodigal Son the grace of penance—that is, self-knowledge, self-condemnation, sorrow for the past, conversion, self-accusation, and the will to amend one's life. We have here then, I say, a divine delineation of what it is. Let us take another example.

There was in Jerusalem one who was rich, and abounded in all things. She possessed also the fatal gift of beauty, which has been eternal death to tens of thousands. She was living in wealth and luxury and enjoyment, and, as the Apostle said, was "dead while she lived." She decked herself out in gold and in fine apparel, like the daughters of Jerusalem of whom the Prophet Isaias says, that they were haughty, and walked with their necks stretched out, with wanton glances in their eyes, and making a noise with their feet, and walking with a mincing step, with the affectation of an immodest and luxurious life. She was known to be a sinner and was notorious in the city. On a day—

we know not when, we know not where, for it is not written—she chanced, as we say, to light upon the presence and to hear the voice of our Divine Redeemer. It may be that it was in the Temple where He daily taught. It may be she had gone up to the Temple in all the bravery and all the ostentation of her apparel, not to worship the Holy One of Israel, but from curiosity, and to be seen, and to show herself to men. But she found herself in the presence of One whose calm dignity abashed her.

At first, it may be, she resisted the sound of the voice; but there was something in it which thrilled to the depth of the heart. There was something in the still steady gaze of that divine eye which she could not escape. A shaft of light cut her heart asunder, and an illumination showed her to herself, even as God saw her, covered with sins red as scarlet, and, as the leper, white as snow. She went her way with the wound deep in the heart—a wound which could never be healed save only by the hand that made it. She went to her own home, no doubt, and cast over in her mind what she had heard. The gaze that had been fixed upon her and the sound of that voice were still in her memory. She could escape them nowhere. No doubt there was a conflict going on day after day, and her old companions, her evil friends, and the manifold dangers of life came thick about her as before; but she had no soul for them.

At last, laying aside her finery and ostentation, unclasping the jewels from her head, and with her hair all loose about her—with an alabaster box of ointment, she walked through the streets of Jerusalem before the eyes of men, caring for no one, thinking of no one but of God and her own sins. Hearing that Jesus of Nazareth sat at meat in the house of Simon the

Pharisee, she broke into the midst of the banquet, under the scornful, piercing, indignant eyes that were fixed upon her; without shame, because her only shame was before the eye of God; without fear, knowing what she was, because she had come to know of the love and tenderness of Him who had spoken to her. She stood silent behind Him, weeping. She had the courage even to kiss His feet, to wash them with her tears, to wipe them with the hair of her head; while the Pharisee secretly rebuked our Divine Lord, and asked himself in his heart: "If this man had been a prophet, would He not have known what manner of woman this is? She is a sinner, and He would not have allowed her to touch His feet."

But those feet had in them the healing of sin. The touch of those feet, powerful as the touch upon the hem of His garment, cleansed that poor sinner. He turned, and in the hearing of them all, He said: "Her sins, which are many, are forgiven her, because she has loved much." Here is an example of the grace of penance; and an example not of penance only, but of perfect and full absolution given in a moment; more than this, of a complete restoration of purity given to the most fallen. In token of that absolution and of that restoration, privileges were granted to Mary Magdalen beyond others. She, out of whom Jesus cast seven devils, was the one who stood at the foot of the cross with the Immaculate Mother of God. It was she who had kissed His feet at that supper who afterwards anointed them, and wound them in the fine linen for His burial. It was she, the greatest of sinners, who, next after His Immaculate Mother, saw Him before all others when He arose from the dead; and these tokens of the love of Jesus to penitents, and to the greatest of penitents, have been followed in the kingdom of Heaven with a glory proportioned to her sorrow and to her love. Mary Magdalen is set forth forever as an example of the grace of penitence, and of the perfect absolution of the most Precious Blood.

But perhaps you will say, she had never known our Saviour. She committed all her sins before she came to the knowledge of His love. I have known Him, and therefore the sins I have committed I have committed against the light; and my sins are more ungrateful than hers, and are therefore guiltier, and I have less hope of pardon. Let us see, then, if there be another example. Is there an example of any friend, who had been highly privileged, greatly blessed, who had known everything, who had received all the light and grace which came from the presence and the words of our Divine Saviour in those three years of His public life—is there any such who afterwards sinned against Him?

There was one to whom the light of the knowledge of the Son of God was first revealed by the Father in Heaven. There was one who was First of all the Apostles, because of this illumination of faith, and to whom our Divine Lord said: "I say unto thee, thou art Peter, and upon this Rock I will build My Church; and the gates of Hell shall not prevail against it: and unto thee will I give the keys of the kingdom of Heaven; and whatsoever thou shalt bind on earth shall be bound in Heaven; and whatsoever thou shalt loose on earth shall be loosed in Heaven." This friend, preferred above all others, dignified above all others, protested to his Master: "Though all men should forsake thee, yet will not I. I am ready to go with thee to prison and to death. Though all men shall deny thee, I will never deny thee." (*Luke* 22:33). He had the courage to draw his sword in the garden, and cut off the ear of the servant of the high priest; yet this man three times denied his Master. He denied him utterly: "I never knew the Man. I am not of His disciples." And with cursing and swearing he renounced his Lord.

Here, then, is the ingratitude and the sin of a cherished friend. But on that night he went out, and he wept bitterly; and his bitter tears upon that night of sin obtained for him not only perfect absolution in the evening of the first day of the week, but the power of absolving the sins of others, sinners like himself. "Receive ye the Holy Ghost; whose sins you shall forgive, they are forgiven unto them." Peter received his own absolution, his own forgiveness, and in that moment he was restored to his dignity as Prince of the Apostles. Though he was upbraided in the gray of the morning on the Sea of Tiberias by the three questions of tender reproof: "Simon, son of John, lovest thou Me, lovest thou Me more than these?" to remind him of his three falls, Peter was restored to more than he had before. He was made head on earth of the Mystical Body of Christ; he died a martyr for his Lord, and he reigns in Heaven by his Master's side.

We have here again an example of the grace of penance; and what do we see in it? Just the same sorrow, self-accusation, reparation as before. Here is the virtue and grace of penance; what, then, is the Sacrament? This grace of penance is as old as the world: it is to be found everywhere where the Holy Spirit works in the hearts of men, if they are faithful and correspond with it. What, then, is the meaning of the Sacrament? Our Lord has instituted a Divine Sacrament, in which He gives the absolution of His most Precious Blood to those that accuse themselves. He instituted it on that night, when He spoke the words with which I began; and the reason for which He instituted it is this—that we may have something more than our self-assurance on which to depend for the hope of our absolution. The Pharisee in the Temple, who stood afar off and said, "God, I thank thee that I am not as other men are—extortioners, unjust, adulterers, or even as this publican" (*Luke* 18:11)—that Pharisee absolved himself; but his absolution was not ratified in Heaven. And so it is often among men.

There are men who absolve themselves all the day long. They forget the sins of their childhood, boyhood, youth, and manhood—ay, the sins of last year, the sins of yesterday; and, having a slippery treacherous memory of their own sins, though retentive and tenacious of the sins of other men, they are perpetually absolving themselves, and assuring themselves that they are pardoned and forgiven before God. There cannot be a state more dangerous, delusive, or fatal; and in order to guard us from this, our Divine Lord has instituted a Sacrament, in which to assure us of our absolution, in which our absolution is a judicial act, an authoritative sentence, an act pronounced by one who is impartial, and who has authority. We are not left to absolve ourselves; we are absolved in the name and by the power of Jesus Christ by a judge empowered by Himself.

Moreover, for our preparation for that Sacrament there is actual grace given; and that grace is the grace of the Holy Ghost, having two effects: first, to give us light to know ourselves more truly, and thereby to understand, to count up, to measure, and to appreciate our sins and the gravity of them; and secondly, that same grace enables us to be contrite, and to make the acts of sorrow. Our Lord instituted the Sacrament; thus

He took the grace of penance which was working from the beginning of the world, and incorporated it in a visible sign: and He communicates His absolution to those who come for it, as He gives the Bread of Life to those who receive Holy Communion at the altar.

Every Sacrament, as you know, is an outward sign of inward grace. It has what is called the form and the matter. What, then, is the form of the Sacrament of Penance? It is these words: "I absolve thee from thy sins." But who can forgive sins except God only? Is it the priest? Do you imagine for one moment that the Holy Catholic Church is—I will not say so superstitious, but is so dull of heart, so dark of understanding as either to believe or teach that it is the man who absolves? It is the office that absolves; and what is the office? The priesthood of Jesus Christ Himself. There are not two, there is but one Priest and one priesthood; and the priesthood that we bear is the participation of that one priesthood of Jesus Christ Himself. What we do, we do not of ourselves. It is He who does it by us. It is simply ministerial on our part. Absolution is given solely and entirely by His power. When at the altar we say, "This is My Body, this is My Blood," do we speak in our own name? Is it possible that anybody with Catholic books before them can be either so dull of sight, or so dull of understanding? There is but one Absolver, Jesus Christ Himself; but He has ten thousand ministers on earth, through whom He applies His Precious Blood to souls that are truly penitent. The act of absolution is His.

Such, then, is the form; next, what is the matter? There are two kinds of matter: there is the matter which is called remote, and the matter which is called proximate. The remote matter of the Sacrament is the sins that we have committed. It is called remote for this reason—they may be the sins of our childhood, a long way off; the sins of our youth, long forgotten, but now at last remembered; the sins that we have committed, and have long hesitated to confess; all these are remote from the present moment, because they are a long way off in our past life; or if they were only of yesterday, still they are not present now. Proximate matter is that state of heart which we must bring with us at the moment, then and there; it is the penitent's contrition, confession of sins, and willingness to make satisfaction.

Now the remote matter is of two kinds. First, there is the necessary matter which we are bound to confess under the pain of eternal death; and there is what is called the voluntary matter, which it is good, wholesome, safe, and better to confess, though it is not of absolute necessity. Now the first means all mortal sins committed after Baptism. As we know of no revealed way in which the mortal Original Sin in which we are born can be absolved except by Baptism, so we know of no other revealed way whereby mortal actual sins committed after Baptism can be absolved, save only by the Sacrament of Penance.[1] You will remember the principles which I laid down in the first and second lectures on these subjects on which I have spoken to you—how one mortal sin separates the soul from God. A soul separated from God is dead; and therefore it is a necessity that every mortal sin we have committed should be confessed and absolved. The voluntary matter is our venial sins.

As to venial sins, there are two reasons why it is good to confess them. The first is because, as I showed you, venial sins may easily pass into mortal sins. Sometimes, through the self-love which is in us, we do not distinguish between them; and we consider what God knows and sees to be mortal to be only venial, and in this we may make dangerous mistakes. Again, to promote humility, self-accusation, sorrow, and therefore the grace of perseverance, and to renew our peace with God, it is good to accuse ourselves of everything we know we have committed since our last confession, even in the least—even in the venial sins of omission of which I lately spoke. It is safer, better, and more wholesome to confess these sins of omission, and to ask God to forgive them; nevertheless, it is quite true that these sins, when they are venial, are not of necessary confession.

Well, the proximate matter means the state of the heart, mind and will. If any man were to kneel down in the confessional, and accuse himself without sorrow for his sins, he would commit another sin. It would be an act of sin in itself. It would be a sacrilege to come and attempt to receive that Sacrament without the proper dispositions, that is, without being worthy; and the man who has no sorrow for sin is not worthy. Nevertheless, it is not necessary that this sorrow be felt with the emotions; rather, it is the decision of the will to hate and turn away from the sins one has committed.

Next, there must be a decision of the will to amend one's life. If a man come and ask for pardon, even were he to accuse himself perfectly, without having a resolved purpose not to sin again—which includes avoiding the occasions of sin—that man would commit a sacrilege. Therefore, the heart and mind must be sorrowful, and the will resolved not to commit sin again. You will say: "How can a man say this, knowing his weakness and instability?" The answer is that if any man sincerely resolves not to sin, and is conscious of his own weakness, and afraid of it, that is a true and a good resolution—and God will accept it, even though afterwards through suddenness or subtlety of temptation he should be cast down. At the time, he was perfectly sincere in his resolutions, and that is all that God requires.

Now, the Sacrament of Penance has three effects, which is indeed one threefold effect. The first is that it absolves or looses the soul from the bond of sin. We are using metaphors; to bind and to loose is a metaphor. What is it that binds a soul? It is the sin. And what is the sin? I told you in the beginning. It is the variance or the opposition of the will against God; it is the crookedness and perversity of the will, resulting in the palsy of the heart, the darkness of the conscience, and, in the case of mortal sin, carrying with it the penalty of eternal death. This is the bond of sin. Now the Sacrament of Penance takes away our sins and the guilt of our sins, and if we are absolved of *mortal* sin, it cancels out the penalty of *eternal* punishment in Hell (though there remains the debt of temporal punishment to be suffered either on this earth or in Purgatory). This Sacrament gives the grace of the Holy Ghost; and it is the Holy Spirit of God which brings the will back to God by a change wrought upon the will itself.

The second effect of the Sacrament of Penance is that it infuses grace, as it blots out the sin, so that the soul returns to life. That is to say, a man in mortal sin comes to his confession without Charity, without the love of God, for this reason: that a man in a state of mortal sin no longer has Charity or the love of God (which springs from sanctifying grace). Charity or the love of God is the life of the soul; and if he had this life he would not be in mortal sin. The commission of mortal sin extinguishes the Charity or love of God in him, and the soul dies for that reason. He, therefore, when he comes to accuse himself, has nothing left in his soul but Hope and Faith; he hopes to be pardoned, and he believes that God will pardon him if his confession be good. Then, after his act of self-accusation, as he receives his absolution, the grace of Charity is restored to him, the life of the soul is given back, he is united with God once more, he possesses Faith, Hope, and Charity, as he did in his Baptism—as he did before he fell, for the Sacrament puts him back again into the state of grace as at first.

Thirdly, it does something further: it restores the soul to its previous condition. You remember that I told you some time ago that if any man had lived a life of faith, charity, piety, generosity, and good works, and afterwards fell into one mortal sin, all those fruits would be dead upon the tree, because the tree itself was dead. But when he is restored to grace, all those fruits that were once dead revive with the tree also, though to a greater or lesser degree according to the depth of the penitent's contrition. The leaves expand once more in their tenderness and freshness, and the fruits are once more ripe upon the bough. All the supernatural acts of the past life, which were mortified and lost by one mortal sin, come to life again; and when they are restored to life, the merit of every such act—and you remember what I told you merit is, the link between the action and the reward constituted by the promise of God in His free and sovereign grace—all this merit likewise is restored; and with this, also, the supernatural powers of the soul are renewed. The soul in mortal sin had lost its grace, its conscience was blind, its ear was deaf, and its will was weak. Like as our Divine Lord, in His miracles, opened the eyes of the blind, and the ears of the deaf, straightened the feet of the lame, and made the man with the withered hand to stretch it out like the other, so, when the soul is restored by absolution and grace in the Sacrament of Penance, the powers of the soul are again restored. The man is again able to perform acts of supernatural saving Faith, Hope, and Charity, and all the other Christian virtues.[2]

You see, then, what the Sacrament of Penance is. It is the grace of penance enlarged, multiplied, assured, brought within the reach of men, offered all the day long, within the power of everybody. That which in the beginning was unseen and secret, now is embodied visibly in a Sacrament of grace, that men may know where to find the Fountain in which they may wash and be clean.

I can say but few words more. When He instituted, in our behalf, this holy Sacrament out of the tenderness of His love and the superabundance of His grace to sinners, our Divine Lord set no limit whatever to its efficacy. It is like His own Precious Blood. It is powerful and omnipotent to cleanse all sin. He sets no limit; there is indeed a limit, as I will show you, but it is not God who imposes it. There is no sin of any kind, howsoever deep, dark, black as midnight, and often committed, nothing so inveterate, nothing which in the sight of God is so hateful, nothing which to the soul of man is so deadly, that there cannot be absolution for it in the Sacrament of Penance.

Do not for one moment imagine that you have sinned beyond the power of pardon. There is no man who hears me, whatever his sin may have been, who, if he will turn and repent and accuse himself with sorrow, shall not be washed as white as snow. Next, there is no kind of sin that is beyond the reach of absolution. There is no number of sins, however frequent, which shall not be pardoned. Though a man were to go on all his life long—sinning day and night, repeating sins over and over again—yet repenting of them on his deathbed, the Precious Blood shall wash him white as snow. Our Divine Lord has said that "if our brother offend against us seventy times seven, ay, and that in one day, and turn and repent, we are to forgive him." (*Luke* 17:4; *Matt.* 18:22). In saying that, He used a form of speech to show there is no number—there is no numerical limit.

There can only be a moral limit, and a moral limit there is; but what is it? I said before: "All sin and all blasphemy shall be forgiven unto men, save only the blasphemy of the Holy Ghost; that shall never be forgiven in this world or in the world to come." (*Matt.* 12:31, 32). But what is this blasphemy of the Holy Ghost? It is the resistance to the known truth. It is the refusal of the grace of penance. It is the outrage done to the Absolver Himself, the Giver of Life; and that by the impenitence of the sinner. The one only sin which is beyond the reach of absolution, the one only sin which the Precious Blood cannot absolve, is the sin that is not repented of; that is the sole and only sin that shall not be washed as white as snow.

Finally, as our Divine Lord has set no limit to His forgiveness, and as the limit is set by man, and by man only through his own impenitence, so our Divine Saviour has attached to this grant of His pardon only those conditions without which He would cease to be what He is—holy, just, true, and merciful. If He were to require more, He would require more than we can do. If He were to require less, He would violate His own divine perfections. The Sacrament of Penance is the Precious Blood and the pardon of the Precious Blood let down within the reach of the lowest sinner— lower it cannot be; for it is within the reach of all. The conditions which are attached to it are the following. The first is that we be sorry. God would cease to be God—He would cease to be just, holy, and pure—if He were to forgive those who are not sorry for their sins, who still love them, and are therefore at variance with Him, and at variance with His perfections.

Secondly, we must come to Him. If the Prodigal had lingered in the far country, his father could not have fallen on his neck. If Mary Magdalen had not broken into the midst of that banquet, she would not have heard the words of her absolution. We, then, must come to Him. He has commanded us to come. He has said: "I am the way, the truth, and the life. No man cometh unto the Father but by me." (*John* 14:6). And the way He has ordained for penitents to come to Him is in self-accusation, in the Sacrament of Penance.

Then, when we come to Him, we must accuse ourselves honestly, truly, sincerely. There must be no excusing, no painting of the face. We cannot paint the heart, and God looks at the heart, and not at the countenance. Our accusation must be truthful to the very last. Every mortal sin that we have committed from our earliest childhood, so far as we remember, it must be at some time confessed before it can be absolved. It is not requiring much of the sinner that he should come and say what is his disease, that he should show his wounds, and his miseries, and the symptoms of death that are upon him. The physician requires no more for healing, and he can require no less.

And, He requires of us a steadfast resolution to sin

no more, and to avoid the occasions of sin—of which I will speak hereafter—that is, a steadfast change of the will, retracing the variance and the opposition of the will against His will, and a sincere resolution to offend Him no more. Less than this He could not require; and more than this He does not.

Lastly, there must be a willingness to make satisfaction to God for the offense we have committed against Him. True it is, that finite man cannot make up for an offense to the Infinite God; yet there is a certain measure of expiation which God requires of man for his every sin, even though the guilt of that sin be washed away in the Precious Blood of our Saviour in the Sacrament of Penance. This expiation, made in the state of grace, by a living branch in union with the Vine which is Christ, possesses a divine, supernatural value. And we know, as I have said before, that those sins which are not expiated on earth, remain to be expiated in Purgatory.[3] Here, then, are the conditions: sorrow for having offended God; the coming to Him in His own way; true self-accusation; steadfast resolution to sin no more, and the willingness to make satisfaction.

O, dear brethren, anticipate the Day of Judgment. Be beforehand with it. That day is coming, inevitably coming, as the rising of tomorrow's sun. The day is not far off when the Great White Throne will be set up, and we shall stand before Him; and the eyes, that are as a flame of fire, will search us through and through; and not His eyes alone, but the eyes of all men will be upon us; and the ears of men will hear that which the accuser will say against us in that day. There will be no secrecy then; no hiding of our sins, nothing concealed from God, or from that multitude which is around the Great White Throne.

What does He require of you now? The Great White
Throne is veiled in His mercy. In the holy Sacrament of
Penance He sits as the Judge, not arrayed in the splen-
dors which will dazzle and blind us at the Last Day,
but as the Good Shepherd, and as the Good Physician,
the Friend of sinners, who is "come not to call the just,
but sinners to repentance." There He sits in His mercy.
Come to Him, then, one by one. Be beforehand with
the Day of Judgment. That which you confess now will
be blotted out and forgiven in that day. That which you
hide now will be in the book of God's remembrance,
laid up for a record in the day of the great assize. It is
not much He requires of us—to come and tell it in the
ear of one man in His stead—a man bound under a
seal, which, if he were to break, he would commit a
mortal sin of sacrilege; a seal which no priest would
break, even if it cost him his life upon the spot. If it be
painful to you, if shame cover your face, offer up the
pain and the shame as a part of the penance, as Mary
Magdalen in the midst of that great banquet. It is precisely for this purpose: that the salutary pain may be
the medicine of our pride.

Dear brethren, then, be beforehand with the Day of
Judgment, while the day of grace lasts: and come to
Him as you are. Do not say, "I must wait"—do not say,
"I cannot come with all my sins upon me, stained as I
am, covered from head to foot with spots crimson as
blood. I cannot come as I am. Let me wait a little
while. I shall be better and fitter hereafter." Do not
reason thus with yourselves. These are the whispers of
the enemy, who desires to stand between you and your
absolution. Come with all your sins upon you, though
they are more numerous than the hairs of your head,
though they are black as night, though they are beyond

all count and all measure. Come just as you are. If you had a mortal sickness, would you put off going to the physician until the symptoms are abated? The more intense and threatening the symptoms, the faster you will go for counsel and for healing. Do not say to yourselves, "I am so hard-hearted. I have not a tear. I have not the feeling of sorrow." How can you, if you are in sin? It is sin that hardens the heart and dries the eyes.

In the Sacrament of Penance the grace of the Holy Ghost will deepen your sorrow and perhaps even give you the emotion of sorrow. Do not say, "I am so unstable. If I were pardoned today, I should fall tomorrow." Are you more likely to stand tomorrow because you will not be forgiven today? Oh, no.

Dear brethren, whatever be your sins, how many, however guilty, come with them all, like the poor woman who touched the hem of His garment, like the poor Prodigal, barefooted and ragged, when he came back to his father's house. Come as you are, and do not lose time. Time and grace are God's gift: we know not how long they may last. At this moment the Sacred Heart of Jesus bleeds for you on the Cross, yearns for you in Heaven. The father who saw the Prodigal afar off, and who ran to meet him, is the pledge, ay, and the earnest of that yearning fervent love and thirsting desire with which Jesus is waiting to forgive you.

Every soul washed in the Precious Blood is a joy to the Good Shepherd. He knows what is stirring in you. He has seen the strings of your conscience. He has seen the wavering of your will. He has seen the good impulses that have been prompting you. He knows the temptations that are keeping you back, and the aspirations that have been lifting you up towards Him—the longing for strength and courage to cast yourself at His feet, and make your peace with Him. He knows all this. Dear brethren, do not resist Him. Take heed lest you quench those emotions of grace that are within you. How long, how long, how long shall He wait for? Remember His own words: "There is joy in heaven over one sinner doing penance more than over ninety-and-nine just persons that need no repentance." (*Luke* 15:7).

NOTES

1. It is true that *perfect contrition,* or contrition arising from true love of God, procures the remission of even mortal sins without the actual reception of the Sacrament of Penance; however, this contrition must contain, at least implicitly, the intention of receiving the Sacrament at the earliest opportunity. Thus it is indeed true that every mortal sin we have committed must be confessed and absolved. Very often, or even in most cases, our contrition is *imperfect,* arising from a lesser motive such as fear of God's punishments or sorrow over the loss of sanctifying grace. In the Sacrament of Penance, imperfect contrition is sufficient for the forgiveness of sins, including mortal sins. Furthermore, imperfect contrition is sufficient for the remission of mortal sin in the Sacrament of Extreme Unction, if the sick person is not able to make his confession.

2. Yet the soul may be out of the way and the habit of practicing these virtues, and must needs exert itself with diligent efforts, with the help of God's grace, to return these powers to their former strength.

3. The penance assigned by the priest in the Sacrament of Penance— usually the reciting of a few prayers—in most cases constitutes only a very partial expiation.

Sermon VI

TEMPTATION

"Then Jesus was led by the spirit into the desert, to be tempted by the devil."

—Matt. 4:1

The Son of God, who is Incarnate Sanctity and Eternal Life, when He came into the world to redeem mankind, placed Himself in the most intimate contact, possible to His perfections, with sin in the desert, and with death upon the Cross. In the temptation in the desert, Jesus tasted of all the bitterness of sin, except only of its guilt: in His death upon the Cross, the immortal God tasted death for every man. Now I have taken the temptation of our Divine Saviour as the outset of our present thoughts, because in itself it is sufficient proof of what I affirmed some time ago, namely, that to be tempted is not to sin, and that many who are the most tempted are innocent. You will remember I was speaking about the distinctions of sin, when I touched upon the subject of temptation. It was necessary to guard what I was saying, lest those who are tempted, and perhaps sorely and habitually, should lose heart, and begin to fear lest their temptations are personal sins.

Now the example of our Divine Lord shows us that One who is sinless may be the subject of temptation. He suffered temptation for our sakes, just as He suffered death for our sakes. He suffered temptation, in order, as St. Paul says, "that we may have such a high priest, not one who cannot have compassion or be touched with a feeling of our infirmities, but one who was tempted in all things like as we are, yet without sin" (*Heb.* 4:15); and again, that "He suffered, being tempted, that he might know how to succor or give help to those that are tempted." (*Heb.* 2:18). It was that, out of His own personal experience, the Son of God, incarnate in our humanity, might taste of sin in all its bitterness, in all its penalties, save only that which to Him is impossible, the guilt of sin, that so He might be a Saviour full of sympathy with sinners.

And now it is necessary to observe the distinction, which I have drawn with all possible care and precision. Though it is true that temptation is not sin, nevertheless temptation and sin are very nearly allied— they are very like each other, and they may be easily mistaken; secondly, temptations are the occasions of sin; and thirdly, temptations with great rapidity and with great facility pass into sins. For this cause it is necessary with all accuracy to distinguish between them. Perhaps someone will say: "I can quite understand that the Son of God, being man, was capable of being tempted; but that gives me little encouragement, because every temptation presented to His sinless soul was instantly quenched, like as sparks falling upon the face of pure water are immediately extinguished; but when temptations come to me, the sparks are struck upon the touchwood, they fall upon the flax, and upon the dry leaves which are ready to kindle."

There is indeed this difference. The temptations of our Divine Saviour were altogether from without, and none of them from within; our temptations are indeed in great part from without; but a very large part of them, and the worst part of them, are from within. They come up out of our own hearts, they are in our own thoughts, in our own passions, in our own tempers, in our faculties, in our memory—here are the lairs and the haunts of temptation. These are the most dangerous, and the example of our Divine Lord does not reach to what we suffer. Now, nothing is more certain than this, that all the sorrows which come upon a man in life—sickness, pain, bereavements, afflictions, all the crosses he may meet with, losses, disappointments, bankruptcy—all these things are nothing, compared with the bitterness, the keenness, of temptation.

A man may say: "I could bear all these things readily. They come from without; and they have not that which is the special suffering of temptation, the bitterness of sin is not in them. They do not come between me and God. Indeed, the more of suffering and sorrow I have in this world, the more I am driven to the presence of God. They are rods and scourges, driving me nearer and nearer to Him; but my temptations come between me and God. They come and cut me off from Him. They hang like a dark cloud between me and the face of God. They make me feel it to be impossible that God can love me, impossible that I can be saved, impossible that I should not be grieving the Holy Spirit of God all the day long. I am like those who are described in Holy Scripture, who do many things for the best, nevertheless, after all, do not know whether they are the objects of love or hatred."[1] (*Eccles.* 9:1).

Now, I dare say there is not one of you who does not know and feel what Holy Scripture calls "the wound of his own heart." The wound of a man's heart is the great master fault, or the besetting sin, or the three or four

besetting sins, such as pride, anger, irritability of
temper, jealousy, envy, slothfulness, and many others
which I need not specify. I desire to meet the objection
of such persons, and I desire to show and to prove, that
it is quite possible that a man who suffers all the day
long from temptations of this kind, may, nevertheless,
in the sight of God, be innocent; and so far as those
temptations go, he may be perfectly guiltless. I do not
say that this is a common case, but I say it may be; and,
therefore, everyone may, if he will only be faithful to
the rules I will hereafter try to lay down, take to himself, at least in part, this consolation.

1. First of all, then, temptation is inevitable. Until we
have put off our mortality, until corruption is turned
into incorruption, we shall be assailed by temptation.
To be tempted is simply to be man; to be man is to be
tempted. In Holy Scripture, in the book of Genesis, we
read these words, that "God did tempt Abraham" (*Gen.*
22:1); but in the Epistle of St. James we read, "Let no
man when he is tempted say that he is tempted by
God." (*James* 1:13). This seems to be a contradiction—
but it is not, because the word "tempt" is a word of perfectly neutral signification. It does not necessarily mean
"tempt with evil"; it simply means to "try"—"God did
try Abraham"; for God puts us on our trial, and that in
two ways. He either by His providence sends us a
variety of afflictions, or crosses, or losses, or contradic-
tions, by which He tries what our spirit is; or, secondly,
He permits that Satan should try us, as He permitted
Satan to try and afflict Job. Therefore, when it is said
that God "tempts," it means that God tries us; but the
other signification is an evil one; for all the temptations
that come from Satan are evil in themselves. He never
tempts any man to good, unless some accidental good

may be the occasion of evil. Now, it is in this latter sense that I am going to speak—that is, of our being tried by evil, tried by Satan. God overrules even the temptations of Satan for our benefit, as I will show.

I say, then, that these temptations are inevitable, and that for this reason: from the time when the Dragon and his angels were overcome by Michael and his angels in Heaven, and Satan was cast out with his evil angels upon earth, from that moment to this there has been warfare round about us. Remember that Satan is an angel created with an intelligence and a will and a power far exceeding that of man.

There is something satanic in the contempt and the ridicule with which men treat Satan. I say it is satanic, because it is a satanic illusion to make men cease to fear him, or cease even to believe in him. He is never more completely master of a man than when the man ridicules his existence—when, as we hear in these days, men say, "There is no devil." The man most under the power of the tempter is he who does not believe in the existence of his enemy. His enemy is round about him day and night, and under his feet. Satan, being of angelic nature, has an angelic intelligence greater than that of man, pervaded by craft and by subtilty. He has also an angelic will mightier than ours, pervaded by an intensity of malice. He has also a power greater than ours, which is always exerted out of jealousy against those who are redeemed in the Precious Blood of Jesus Christ. It was not shed for him; and he is laboring, therefore, day and night, without ceasing, to destroy those who are the heirs of salvation.

There are two titles given to Satan in Holy Scripture: Our Lord called him "the prince of this world" (*John* 14:30), and St. Paul calls him "the god of this world"

(*1 Cor.* 4:4); and therefore we have closely surrounding us, like an atmosphere, the world of which he is the prince, and, I may say, the sanctuary of which he is the god. For what is the world? It is the intellectual and moral state of the race of mankind without God, pervaded, darkened, falsified, and corrupted by the influence of Satan into the likeness of his own malice. Therefore, Holy Scripture declares that the world is an enemy of God, an immutable enemy; that the world can never be reconciled with God, or God with the world; that the world can never be purified; that even the waters of Baptism only save individuals out of the world; and that the world itself will never be saved, but will be burned up by fire.

Now, this world signifies the tradition of the sin of mankind, the worldwide corruption of human nature by the sins of the flesh and the sins of the spirit, with all their falsehood, impiety, and malice against God. This hangs in the atmosphere of the world: outside Christendom it reigns supreme; inside Christendom it has entered again, like as in the time of pestilence; the very air of our dwellings, after all the care we can bestow, is infected. Even among baptized nations the spirit of the world, wafted from without, and arising up again under our feet from the corrupt soil of human nature, is perpetually renewing itself; and we live surrounded by an atmosphere in which all forms of truth are distorted, and where illusions are presented on every side, so that men are misled, and are turned away from God and from His laws. We live in the midst of such a world, and that world we renounced in our Baptism—"the world with all its pomps"; nevertheless, it has a perpetual action and influence upon every one of us. There is what is called the worldly spirit, which enters with the greatest subtilty into the character of even good people; and there is what is called the time-spirit, which means the dominant way of thinking and of acting which prevails in the age in which we live; and these are powerful temptations, full of danger, and in perpetual action upon us.

Then, thirdly, we carry our temptations about us. We have every one of us the three wounds of Original Sin: ignorance in the understanding; turbulence in the affections, so that they become passions; instability and weakness in the will. The soul is wounded with those three wounds; and nevertheless it is in perpetual motion in thought, word, and deed, save only during the time of sleep. In our waking hours our nature is in unceasing activity, and in perpetual anarchy too, except in those who, being guided by the Spirit of God, are under the influence of grace and conformed to the truth. The thoughts, tempers, affections, passions of the heart, are in a state of ceaseless turbulence, so that the Holy Ghost by the Prophet describes the heart in these words: "The wicked are like a raging sea which cannot rest, casting up mire and dirt." (*Is.* 57:20). As the sea casts up from its depths the soil under the waters, so the perpetual activity of the heart is casting up the passions and the concupiscences that lie within it. This description applies in its measure to every one of us. We are all in this state; and, therefore, the temptations of Satan, the temptations of the world which are without us, and the temptations from our own heart within— these three temptations are inevitable. We cannot escape them.

Every one of us singly stands between two spirits— there is the Spirit of God on the one side, there is the spirit of Satan on the other; and the human spirit, that is, the soul with its intelligence, heart, and will, stands between. These two spirits, of God and of Satan, are in perpetual conflict round about us and for us—the spirit of Satan striving to pervert, to delude, and to cast us down; the Spirit of God perpetually guiding, strengthening, and upholding us. The thoughts of Satan are infused into us, and also the lights of the Holy Ghost—and sometimes we do not know the one from the other. We sometimes mistake the false lights of Satan for the lights of truth. We sometimes fancy that the lights of truth which come are only temptations. Sometimes we imagine our own human thoughts to be the thoughts and the lights of God; and so we deceive ourselves. We are in this constant state of temptation, which is common to all men.

2. Next, the universality of this temptation is so great, that there is no state of man that is not visited by it. Take, for example, sinners, those that live voluntarily in sin. Satan tempts them; they are the subjects of constant satanic temptation; but be sure that they are not the chief subjects of his temptations, for this reason: they are his servants already, they are already doing his will, they already share his own mind, they already love those evils to which he tempts them. Satan leaves his own servants to do their work for him; they have united themselves with his evil angels.

When our Lord was tempted in the wilderness, it was but the lifting of the veil, and the making visible of that which invisibly is taking place every hour and every moment round about us. "We wrestle not with flesh and blood," as the Apostle says, "but with principalities and powers, and spiritual wickedness in high places" (*Eph.* 6:12); that is, with the whole hierarchy of fallen angels round about us. They are mingling among evil and

wicked men; the evil and the wicked have united themselves to their allegiance, and Satan leaves them
alone—they are doing his work.

The blasphemer is not tempted to blasphemy. Why
should he be? He blasphemes already. The unbeliever
is not tempted to unbelief—he has lost his faith. The
scoffer is no longer tempted to scoffing—he scoffs
enough already to satisfy even the "god of this world."
So I might go on with every other kind of sin. They
have become the members of the "mystery of impiety."
(*2 Thess.* 2:7). Just as all faithful children of God are
members of Christ, and the mind and the will and spirit
of Jesus Christ descend into them; and being living
members of the Mystical Body of Christ, they are
united to their Divine Head, so the wicked and sinful
are pervaded, as it were, by the mind and the spirit and
the will and the malice of Satan: they are, as it were,
members of Satan, members of what we might call the
"mystical body" of Satan, and are united to their
satanic head, and are under his guidance.

But, next, if any one of them strives to return to God,
he becomes the subject of a twofold temptation. Satan
follows up every deserter who leaves his camp, and he
follows him with an intensity of redoubled malice. He
multiplies all his temptations. Those by which he fell
before, when he tries to rise again and to escape from
them, Satan doubles their power and their effect. He
never gives him rest. If any of you have tried to break
off a fault, I have no doubt you have found that you
have been more tempted to that same fault from the
very time you began to master it. Need I tell you why?
Before, you were swimming with the stream; but when
you tried to break off that fault you were swimming
against the stream, and you felt the strength of the

stream against you. That is to say, you were going onward before the temptation until you turned from sin,
then you felt the full force of temptation against you
like the stream and current of a river; and that stream
and current was doubled by the malice of the tempter.

He is not only very strong in his temptations, but he
is very subtle; and when men begin to break off sins of
one kind, he will leave them perfectly quiet on that
side, and will tempt them on the other to something else
which is altogether unlike their former faults. As, for
instance, if any man has been tempted to gross sins and
has gained the mastery, he will find himself tempted to
spiritual sins, which, casting him down, will bring him
back to where he was before. Be sure of it, whoever
begins, for example, to mortify such a sin as excess in
food, if he gains the mastery, will find himself tempted
perhaps to some spiritual sin, such as anger, ill-temper,
or, it may be, vainglory at what he has achieved. It is
all one; what does it matter? There are seven capital
sins, of which three may be said to be of the body and
four of the soul, but they all can cast the soul into Hell;
and if a man perishes by spiritual sin, he is just as certainly condemned to eternal death as if he perishes by
the grossest sins of the flesh. Satan in his subtlety
knows this, and follows up every man that has turned
away from him; and those who turn from him and strive
to convert their souls to God are his special objects of
temptation.

Even those whom we call servants of God, who have
really turned away from Satan and are confirmed in a
life of faith and piety—they too have special temptations. For instance, when Satan sees any soul escape
out of his hands, and no longer under the dominion of
the grosser sins of the body, he changes himself into the

likeness of an angel of light. He knows that the grosser forms of temptation will have no more power, that they will be disgusting and alarming, that they will repel and will drive the soul from him; and therefore he changes himself into an angel of light. He comes as a messenger of peace and a preacher of justice and a teacher of purity: and then he will stimulate and excite the imprudent to strain after perfections of penance and perfections of prayer and mystical reaches of the spiritual life, which we read of no doubt in saints, but such as are yet far out of the grasp of those who are beginning to serve God. Nevertheless, these things are sufficient to turn the head and to infuse vainglory, and to call men off from the humble practice of daily duty, and make them climb and clamber up into high places, where they have not the head to stand, and at last they fall through a spiritual intoxication.

So also, those who have turned away from him he tempts to a censorious judgment of others. When they have light to know their own faults and their eyes are opened to discern sin, the use they make of their enlightened eyes is very often to be quick and searching to find the faults of their neighbors; and by turning their eyes outwardly, which are intended to be turned inwardly, they range to and fro, finding out and censuring the faults of other people, and perpetually committing rash judgments in their hearts, and very often, sins of detraction with their tongues.

There is also another temptation, even for those that are advancing far in the way of perfection. Spiritual writers tell us that there is a temptation which they call "the storm in the harbor"; that is, as a ship which has passed through a tempestuous sea and has come at last into the haven of rest, and is lying calmly over its anchors, may yet be struck by lightning or by a sudden squall, and may founder even in the port of safety; so spiritual pride, spiritual self-love, vainglory at our own imagined perfection, may wreck us at last.

By looking at ourselves in the glass, by reading the lives of the saints until we believe we are saints, by filling our mind with disproportionate and strained imaginations, and then applying them to ourselves: by dreaming that we are that which we can describe, and that there is an aureola, a crown of light hanging over our heads, we may finally cast ourselves down from God. These imaginings and delusions, which come from a profound self-love, and as profound a want of self-knowledge, will turn the heads and the consciences even of those who have escaped from grosser sins, and make them like Simon the Pharisee, who, being blind to his own faults, and censorious of the faults of others, was, in comparison with poor Mary Magdalen, a sinner before the eyes of our Lord: or like the Pharisee in the Temple, who, after thanking God he was not like other men, went down to his house not justified as the poor Publican was.

Therefore we see that temptations are inevitable and universal; and whether you are only penitents or on the way to be saints, do not expect to be exempt from them. Remember, then, that "there is nothing come upon you," as the Apostle says, "but that which is common to man; and God will make also an issue, or a way of escape, so that you may be able to bear it." (*1 Cor.* 10:13). No temptation is a perfect circle. If indeed the circle of temptation were complete, there would be no way out of it. God never permits any temptation to be a perfect ring; there is always an outlet, always a break out of which the soul with safety may escape.

3. There is still another reason why temptation is not sin. However much you may be tempted, whether it be to deadly (mortal) sins or to lighter, it matters not—those temptations will never be imputed to you as sins unless you willingly consent to them. This is the way of escape which is always open, the sure and certain issue by which every soul may pass, even out of a furnace heated sevenfold. You remember, some time ago we laid down as the essential condition of sin, that it is an evil act contrary to the will of God, with knowledge of the intellect, with the consent of the will, and with the consciousness of what we are doing. Now that one rule will precisely distinguish between sins and temptations. St. Paul, in the seventh chapter of the Epistle to the Romans, says: "The good I would, I do not; the evil that I would not, that I do. I consent to the law of God in the inward man; but I find another law in my members, warring against the law of my mind, and bringing me into captivity to the law of sin which is in my members. So if I do the evil that I would not, it is no more I, but sin that dwelleth in me." (*Rom.* 7:15-20). Therefore, St. Paul distinguishes between the indwelling "sin" of his nature (that is, the disordered motions of concupiscence, both physical and spiritual) and himself. He says: "It is no more I." Why is it no more himself? Because his will had no part nor lot in that inward "sinfulness" or concupiscence.

The actions that we do may be distinguished, therefore, into those that are deliberate, and those that are not deliberate, or, as it is called, indeliberate. This distinction will precisely draw the line. A deliberate action of sin is what I have described—with knowledge, consent, and consciousness. An indeliberate action is that in which these elements are wanting. But you will say: "How is that possible?" It is most possible. When we are out in the sun, we feel the warmth by no act of our own. If the wind blows cold, we feel chilled by no act of our own will. All round about us, and all the day long, the images of the world fill the eye, and yet we can only look at one thing at a time. Though we see a thousand, we can only look at one: and that one we look at with the act of our will; but all the rest simply fall upon our passive sight. We go through the streets, we hear a multitude of words to which we do not listen—we know their meaning as they fall upon our passive ear. Now all these are what I may call indeliberate acts. There is no action of the will in them: and we can no more hinder ourselves from seeing and hearing than from being hot or cold. The thoughts that are in us are set in motion; and the thoughts weave their associations. The memory revives, and gives up the images of the past; and the imagination adds to them—and this process goes on at all hours; for in truth our minds are never at rest. Ay, even in sleep we dream; which is a reason to believe that, though the body is perfectly suspended in its conscious action, the mind is never suspended. Now a great deal of this mental action may indeed become sin if we consent to it; but it is not sin if we do not consent to it: and that for the following reason.

The will, as I have already said before, is the rational appetite of the soul. It is the desire we have in us, guided by reason, choosing and determining what we shall pursue. But round about the will there is, first of all, a circle of affections, which, as God first created them in the Garden of Paradise, were all pure. Round about the affections are the passions, which, as sin has wounded them, are all of them somewhat in disorder;

and round about the passions are the senses—sight and
hearing, taste and touch—these are the inlets through
which sin gains entrance. The Prophet says: "Death
climbs up by the windows" (*Jer.* 9:21); which spiritual
writers interpret of sin finding its entrance through the
senses—through the open eyes, the open ears—which
are like the windows of the soul standing wide.

Satan has no power at all to enter into the soul
against our will. The Holy Ghost can enter into the
soul, because He is the Creator of the soul, and the
Uncreated Spirit of God pervades all creatures. He is
the Searcher of the heart, because He pervades the
whole heart. He knows it all, because He is present in
all; but Satan cannot enter the heart as the Holy Ghost.
All that he can do is stand without, watching at the
windows, and casting in "the fiery darts." (*Eph.* 6:16).
These "fiery darts" are the temptations which enter
through the senses, fall upon the passions, and kindling
them, disorder the affections, and through them affect
the will; but if the will does not consent, the presence of
any amount of temptation may be mere suffering, and
however intense, it will not be sin.

So that the way to distinguish between what is
temptation and what is sin is to ask yourselves, Do you
welcome it? Do you open the door? Do you throw up
the window? Do you invite it to come in and dwell? Or
do you say: "The Lord rebuke thee—get thee behind
me, Satan"? How do you receive these temptations?
When the fiery darts are cast in by the window, do you
trample them out or leave them to kindle, till by the
eye, or the ear, the memory, and the imagination, they
are set on fire?

You feel as if a touch had moved you; as for example, what is a fit of anger but a sudden touch of fire,

which comes before we have a moment to deliberate?
An offensive answer, or some insolent gesture, or something done in a way to provoke the natural passion of
wrath, will immediately elicit our anger. It is in our
nature; we cannot help it. As on striking a flint you
strike a spark, so on striking human nature, anger immediately responds; and that first emotion of anger is
not sinful. It is a sin, if I deliberately welcome it and
say, "O, this is just come in time. This is just what I
wanted. I have a will to be angry." If you heap on fuel,
by thinking of the offence that has been committed, and
stir the fire to make it burn more fiercely, then indeed
you make it your own. I might give other examples, but
you can find them for yourselves, because every one of
the seven capital sins may be taken in like manner. I
have given the example of one only, to save time, and
also because it is better that you make them for yourselves.

Another certain test whether it is temptation or sin is
this: does the presence of the temptation give you
pleasure, or pain? Do you feel rather gratified by being
stirred up to a sense of resentment, or does it give you
pain that you have lost your calmness? If you have
pleasure in it, then most assuredly you have been con-
senting; if it gives you pain, then as certainly it is contrary to your will. You know it to be contrary to the law
of God, to the example of Jesus Christ; you feel it to be
contrary to His meekness, His charity, His love, His
compassion, and His generosity, and you feel inwardly
grieved and pained with yourself that you are so unlike
Him. You know it to be contrary, I will say, to the holiness of God and the purity of your own soul; and
therefore you hate the temptation when it comes. You
strive against it, you reject it, you pray God to rebuke

the presence of the tempter and bruise him under your feet; then you may be well satisfied that all this is a temptation, and not a sin.

I will not say that there may not be some adhesion of your affections, some internal contact as it were, which for a moment puts you in danger; but the example of the first Adam, who, when he was tempted, was sinless, and of the second, who was God, are proofs to us that fiery temptations which we hate may come upon innocent persons.

4. All the manifold temptations of life are used by God for these two purposes: first, to try us, as I have said, and to increase our merit, and therefore our reward; and secondly, to sanctify the soul—out of the very temptations themselves God creates the discipline of sanctification. As to the first, you understand what merit is. We took care to distinguish and define with all precision what is the meaning of merit. It does not mean that we as creatures can snatch by right anything out of the hands of God; but that God has promised He will attach to certain actions a certain reward of His own sovereign grace.

Well, a man is tempted to anger, ambition, falsehood, or whatever you will—if he resists those temptations as a good soldier of Jesus Christ, he proves himself to be faithful and fearless in his warfare. If he resists the temptations to sloth, indulgence, and pleasure, which prevail over softer natures, he shows himself to be a child of God, and a faithful friend to his Divine Friend. He proves that he will neither be scared nor bribed to give up his fidelity; and therefore, every such act of resistance to temptation is, first of all, an act of faith. It is done for motives of faith, it is done because we appreciate the goodness and love of God. We make a deliberate choice between God and the temptation; and we put our foot on the temptation, that we may hold fast by God. Every single act of resisting temptation obtains merit and reward in the sight of God, and they who are the most tempted obtain the most merit, if they faithfully resist; so that the life that is harassed and buffeted with temptations without ceasing, if we persevere, is laying up perpetually more and more of merit before God, and more and more of reward in eternal life. And every such act of resistance to temptation is an act of love to God. Though we say nothing, our actions are always breathing upwards. "O my God, I would rather die than do this; and that, for Thy sake." And every time we so act, God interprets it as an act of love to Himself. He knows us as our Lord knew Peter, when he said, "Lord, thou knowest all things—thou knowest that I love thee." (*John* 21:17).

And once more. It is an act of self-mortification. We are mortifying ourselves in the doing of it; and when we mortify ourselves, that act is acceptable in the sight of God. It is the spirit of the Cross, it is an inward crucifixion of the flesh, of its affections and concupiscences, which is the mark of a true Christian. So, as I said before, though a man were walking in the furnace of temptations of every kind, yet if he resists them he is making acts of faith, love, and self-mortification all the day long, increasing his merit before God, and the reward that is laid up for him in Heaven.

5. And the other effect is this—that God uses those very temptations as the means of our sanctification. You remember St. Paul says: "Lest I should be lifted up by the multitude of the revelations, God gave me a thorn in the flesh, a messenger of Satan to buffet me. And for this cause I besought the Lord thrice that it

might depart from me; but he said: my grace is sufficient for thee, for strength is made perfect in infirmity"
(*2 Cor.* 12:7-9)—that is to say, that God made use of
his temptations to perfect him in sanctity.

First of all, He humbles us by them. There is nothing
that gives self-knowledge so much as temptation. Until
a man is tried, nobody knows what is in him. It is an
old proverb. Until a man is tried in temptation, he does
not know himself. He does not know how he will act in
any circumstances, except those of his ordinary life, until he is tried. A man who thinks that he is afar off from
being proud, let him find himself superior to his neighbors; a man who thinks he is in no danger of being
covetous, let him suddenly become rich; a man who
thinks he is in no danger of falling into particular
temptations someday finds himself surrounded by
them—he then learns what he is. Some man who thinks
he could never tell a lie is taken all of a sudden—he
falls from his sincerity. Now temptation teaches us to
know what we are. It throws a light in upon our hearts,
and we learn that before God we are spotted and
stained, and full of tumultuous affections and passions,
with crookedness in the will, darkness in the understanding; and when we come to the knowledge of this, it
breaks down the loftiness of our vainglory. It is a very
unpleasant discovery, but very wholesome—there is
nothing so salutary as for a man to find his own great
instability, that he cannot trust himself. When he has
come to know that he cannot trust himself, then he has
come to know his need of the grace of God; and not till
then.

We read in the life of St. Philip Neri two most in-
structive passages—the one is this: he used to have a
habit of saying, "O my God, keep Thy hand on my

head; for if Thou shouldst let me go, I should break loose and do Thee all manner of harm. The wound in Thy side is large, but I should make it larger." He had such a sense of his own instability, and of his own weakness by nature, that unless the grace of the Holy Spirit sanctified and sustained him, he knew he could not stand; and that if he fell, there was no knowing to what he might go. This grew upon him all his life; so that in a sickness in which they thought he was near to die, he prayed that God would raise him up, that he might do a little more good before he died. He was raised up; but some years afterwards he fell again sick unto death, as all about him believed. And for what did he pray then? "O my God, take me away, that I may do no more harm." He had learned to know himself profoundly. Temptations and trials had made him understand his own nature, and in the sight of God he was becoming humbler and holier every day.

Next, God uses temptations to chastise us; for the temptations which beset us are nine times in ten the effects and the consequences of the faults and sins of our life past. God makes use of the sins and faults we have committed in past years—in childhood, boyhood, youth—to scourge and to humble us in our manhood and old age: and He thereby brings to our memory things we would have forgotten.

Lastly, He uses temptations to awaken and excite in our hearts a hatred of sin; and nothing makes us hate sin so much. When once we have turned away from sin and are no longer consciously guilty, then the hatefulness, hideousness, deformity, the blackness of sin, becomes more and more terrible to us the longer we live. In whose eyes is sin the most hateful? Is it hateful in the eyes of the sinner, or is it hateful in the eyes of

God? In proportion as we are free from sin, in that proportion sin becomes hateful. Just as we grow in light and in grace, in purity, in sanctification, just in that measure sin is hateful to us; and just as we are tempted we learn to know more and more the hatefulness of sin.

We begin first by hating sin in itself, but we do not stop with that abstract hatred. Our next hatred is against what we were once. We remember what we were once upon a time, we recollect what our boyhood or youth was, and there it is before us. The sun, by the photograph, does not take so precise and so terrible a portrait as the conscience, enlightened by the Holy Ghost, takes of our past life. When we see what we once were before the grace of God converted us, the sins we committed in all their darkness and in all their multitude, in all their perversity and in all their ingratitude—when all this is before us and we see our past, the character we once had, hanging like a portrait on the wall, drawn by the pencil of the Holy Ghost, in all its hideousness, we hate ourselves. We hate what we were then; and we hate everything that reminds us of it—the places, the persons, the memorials, the tokens— everything associated with it. Ay, the music and the pictures, and the objects of sight, the books, and tales, and poems, the persons whose influence and whispers were in time past the darkness and downfall of our soul—all this is hateful. And we go on further: our present self, our present character, full of imperfections, ay, and more than that—and the more we know ourself in the light of God's presence, the more we shall come to have that humble sense of self-abhorrence, which, in the sight of God, is the mark of a true penitent.

Now, brethren, I have given you the way to dis-

tinguish between sins and temptations, and I say with
confidence that anybody who can look upon his past
and upon his present, with this feeling of hatred, and
sorrow, and humility, may console himself with the
conviction that whatever temptations beset him from
without, his heart and his will are intensely and firmly
set against these temptations, and that sin has no part in
him: "It is no more I, but sin that dwelleth in me."
(*Rom.* 7:17). I then have given you the reasons, first,
that temptation is inevitable, that temptation is universal, that temptation which is not consented to is not sin,
that temptation resisted is a perpetual increase of merit,
and temptation resisted brings a continual growth of
sanctification.

I have now only two simple counsels to add. All this
is true, subject to two conditions. The one is that we
avoid the occasions of sin. You know what the word
means. There is a difference between an occasion of
sin, and a temptation to sin. A temptation to sin means
a positive danger, present here and now; but an occasion of sin may mean something lawful in itself which
may lead us on to the danger of sin. The occasions may
sometimes be lawful things altogether, innocent things
which, like slippery places in our path, deceive our
tread.

There are three reasons why we are bound to avoid
the occasions of sin. The first is this, that no man, when
he makes his confession kneeling under a crucifix, can
make a good confession, or can escape the risk of a
sacrilegious confession, and no man can receive a valid
absolution, who does not, at the time when he accuses
himself of his sins, make a firm, sincere, and steadfast
resolution to avoid those sins and all that leads to them.
If he has not got the will to give up the occasions which

have caused him in past times to sin, and to commit the very sins of which he is now asking absolution in the presence of God, it is a perfect certainty that he has not the sorrow which is necessary for the sins he has committed.

Now, there are two kinds of occasions: there are some which are called necessary, and some that are called voluntary. The distinction is this: let me suppose for a moment that some of you are tempted to unbelief—I trust in God none of you are—but let me suppose it is possible, and that you have a brother living in the same house with you, who, unfortunately being an unbeliever, pours out all kinds of infidel objections and rationalistic doubts against the revelation of God. You cannot leave your home—you cannot send him out of it—there he is. You are obliged to dwell with him. It is an occasion of temptation to you, and may be an occasion of sin. You cannot get rid of it—it is necessary—there it abides—it is beyond your power and control. God will not call you to an account for not leaving your home under those circumstances. But if you voluntarily and willingly seek conversation on those matters with such a person, that is your voluntary act; and if you do so you are responsible; and unless you steadfastly resolve not to do so, you cannot have absolution of those sins of doubt against faith, into which you have voluntarily plunged yourself. I give this as an example. Apply it in your own heart to every form of sin and of temptation. I will not particularize, but you know perfectly well how easily you may transfer the example I have given to every other kind. It is necessary, then, to your valid absolution that you should steadfastly resolve to avoid every voluntary occasion of sin.

Secondly, it is a part of the reparation due from you

to our Divine Saviour, that, having offended Him, you will not allow yourselves to be drawn back into the same occasions. The spirit of reparation which you owe to Him, after He has absolved you in His Precious Blood, is steadfastly to resist, and watchfully to avoid all those circumstances and occasions which have led you to offend Him before. We read in the book of Acts that the Christians at Ephesus were given to what are called "curious arts" (*Acts* 19:19), omens, magic, superstition, and the like. When they were illuminated by the Faith, they brought their books and burned them in a public place. The people of Milan, after a mission, collected together their foolish books, romances, poetry, bad books and bad pictures, masks, dresses used in masquerades, musical instruments used in vanity and folly, the luxurious and ostentatious ornaments of their persons, and a multitude of other things, as cards, dice, the means of gambling, folly, and loss of time, whatsoever had been to them causes of temptation—they brought them all together into the Piazza del Duomo, and made of them a great bonfire.

I am not going to ask you to make a great bonfire in the streets of London; but what they did materially, you may do spiritually and morally, every one of you. You know, and will find out, what things have been the cause and occasion of sin to you, not only in deed, but in word, in thought, in imagination. Give them up— have nothing to do with them—put them far from you—turn your face from them—put your foot on them; and then, if your temptations recur, you may look up in the face of your Heavenly Father and your Divine Master, and take the peace of knowing that the recurrence of those temptations is chastisement and humiliation, and not your present fault. I do not wish to go into particulars; to do so would lead me into minute details which it is well rather to avoid. It is better rather to give principles and rules, because men of mature mind, persons of Christian faith, will be able to make an application; but I will mention the names of a few of these things.

I ask, first of all, in the use of your food, how much money is wasted in the needless indulgence of the palate? What delicacy and fastidiousness of pleasing the taste is to be found where nobody would suspect it! How much money is wasted in drink; and I am not speaking to you as I should speak if I were in some other part of my flock; but I must say that, even in those who are educated, who belong to the upper region or stratum of society, there is an amount of excessive indulgence in those things which blunts the intelligence, unnerves the will, relaxes the habits of life, deadens the heart, extinguishes the spirit of piety, disturbs the peace of homes, and may lead on to worse. I am bound to tell you openly that, even among persons of education, refinement and of birth, every priest in his experience, and I myself in mine, have known terrible examples of this bondage to drink, which has continued even unto death. How many miserable souls have died, bound in chains of a vice which began perhaps with habits like your own, never suspected it at first, until at last they become virtually indissoluble.

Therefore, I say, in your food, in eating and drinking, be simple, be self-denying. Have the high common sense of Christians; do not care for such things; give no thought to them. The Church enjoins fasting and abstinence; but fasting and abstinence seem dying out. Why? Because people are growing so self-indulgent and so fanciful. Their health will not stand it, and their physician says they cannot endure it, and sometimes even their confessor is besieged until he gives way. There is a law of liberty by which we are to be judged at the Last Day. St. James says: "So speak ye and do as being to be judged by the law of liberty." (*James* 2:12). Now I am appealing to you in the liberty of Christians, in the generosity and gratitude of those who have been redeemed by the Precious Blood of Jesus Christ. I say, deny yourselves in these trivial but dangerous things.

Next, there is a subject too large for me to do more than touch—I mean your dress. I put it first upon the ground of costliness and expense and waste of money; but I may not put it on that only.. Dear brethren, I always avoid entering into details of this matter. I have nothing to do with colors, forms, and fashions—these are things which belong to you; but I have to do with the morals of dress. I have to do with the faults that spring from luxury in dress; and the sin to which luxury and ostentation of dress may lead—that I have to deal with; and what I always try to do is to lay down counsels of broad Christian common sense. I only wish you knew where fashions come from—from some obscure room, in some luxurious and corrupt city, where, by a sort of secret society of folly, rules are laid down and decrees come forth year after year—which are followed with a servility and, I may say, with a want of Christian matronly dignity, so that the foolish fashion that some foolish person has foolishly invented is propagated all over the civilized countries of Europe. From winter to winter and spring to spring our nearest friends are hardly to be recognized. They are dressed up and built up and masqueraded in a way, sometimes, to provoke laughter, or pity, or regret.

I must tell you what once happened to me. I was

walking through one of our parks and I saw three persons, of whom one was dressed according to the novelty of some fashion then coming in, and there followed behind two plain working men. I heard one say to the other, "She only does it to be looked at!" Remember these words of just reproof. That is the estimate which is formed of fashion by the good solid sense of the English people. They pity and despise it. Our forefathers and the women of another age did not bend and undulate with every wind that is wafted over the sea. They dressed and attired themselves as Christian women, taking counsel of their good sense, and attiring themselves as was befitting their station in life, without singularity of plainness, which is one of the affectations of vanity, and without a servile copying of fashion, which is the spirit of this world.

This will give you certain principles, and all I will add is, that there was a time when in Lent people wore black. I do not say it made them more pious or penitent, but I do say it is more in accordance with the time of humiliation and fasting than the gewgaws and glaring colors, peacocks' tails and rainbows, which are to be seen not only in our streets, but round about our altars. There was a custom only a little while ago (and it prevails now in Catholic countries) that no woman came into the house of God except her head was covered by the wearing of a veil, or at least some such covering of the head. It is enjoined in Scripture, and enjoined too by a law on the door of every church in Rome, ay, and at this moment I believe it is still to be found there. I doubt even if the revolution has taken it down. I remember that as long as Rome was the City of the Vicar of Jesus Christ, women were wont to come to the church in fitting attire. I leave this again to you.

Now I have done; this is a subject beyond me, except so far as the morals of dress. All the rest of it I leave to your good sense and to your piety.

I cannot dwell on the other points, but I would say: study well what you can do, in a spirit of liberty and generosity, in the expenditure of money. See how many thousands are in want! The hospitals of London will not contain the one-fifteenth part of those that are mortally sick; and we go about spending money without thinking of those who are dying round about us. There are tens of thousands of children perishing in the streets without Christian education; and we can, with all possible calmness, go and squander our money upon ourselves. I apply the same to your pleasures. I am no rigorist and no puritan, and I love to see people happy and to look on at their innocent enjoyment; but there are some kinds of enjoyments and amusements, some kinds of tastes, which a Christian instinct forbids us to approve. Dear brethren, I hope you will consult Holy Scripture and your conscience, and see what kind of amusement and what kind of pleasure you will look back on calmly from your deathbed, and what kind of enjoyment will give you peace in that hour. Lastly, I would say to you, make a resolution this Lent—for Lent is now finishing. We shall meet again on Good Friday to meditate upon the Passion of our Divine Lord and Saviour Jesus Christ. Make now some one resolution of self-denial out of your full Christian liberty; offer up something as a memorial. I will not prescribe it; choose it for yourselves.

Prayer, piety, watchfulness, self-denial, and purity of heart—these five things will keep your will firm, and if your will be firm it will expel every temptation that enters by the senses, or by the passions, or by the affections, as the flame of a furnace which consumes everything that approaches to its mouth. It will expel and cast out of you all things contrary to your sanctification.

Remember then what our Lord has promised. He suffered temptation that He might have a fellow feeling with you; and you may appeal to Him in your temptations. You may say, "O my Lord, who didst suffer in the desert for my sake, Thou seest the power of this temptation which is upon me. Have pity on me; uphold me, for of myself I cannot stand." He knows how to feel with those who are tempted, and in the midst of your temptations He is perpetually saying to each one of you: "He that overcometh, to him I will give to eat of the tree of life, which is in the midst of the paradise of my God. He that overcometh shall be a pillar in the temple of my God, and he shall go no more out. To him that overcometh I will give to eat of the hidden manna and a white counter, and on the white counter a new name written, which name knoweth no man save only him that receiveth it. He that overcometh shall sit down in my throne, even as I also overcame and am sat down in the throne of my Father." (*Apoc.* 2:7, 17; 3:12, 21).

NOTES

1. See Pages 70 and 71 and Notes 1 and 2, Page 88.

Sermon VII

THE DERELICTION ON THE CROSS

"From the sixth hour there was darkness over the whole earth until the ninth hour; and about the ninth hour, Jesus cried with a loud voice, saying: Eli, Eli, lama sabachthani? that is to say, My God, my God, why hast thou forsaken me?"
—Matt. 27:45-46

It was about the third hour when Jesus set out on the way to Calvary; and it was towards the sixth hour that He reached the place of His Passion. They stripped Him of His garments, and left Him sitting in the cold, withering morning wind; and they began to prepare the crosses of the crucifixion. He sat patiently waiting, in His wounds, upon the top of that hill; and at last, when the cross was ready, He was nailed upon it. The cross was lifted up in the eyes of men; and the Son of God was seen stripped and stretched upon it, hanging by the weight of His whole body upon the nails driven through His hands and feet. They then began to crucify the thieves that were with Him; and some time passed, while He was all alone in His agony.

They were so busy, they were so intent upon this work of death—plying the hammer and the nails in the cruel work of crucifixion—and the people who stood by were so fixed upon the scene of horror, that no one perceived that the sky was growing sickly, that the morning became yellow, that a mist was covering the sun, and that shadows like the shadows of the evening were falling upon the earth. These things they did not perceive, till of a sudden the thick darkness became palpable; they became conscious of it as in a moment. They felt it to be a portent and a sign of the anger of God. Thick darkness covered the hill of Calvary; and the people, one by one, began to stream away from the top of the mountain and from that sight of horror—struck with fear but not with repentance—overwhelmed by horror of that supernatural darkness.

And if there was fear upon Calvary, what was there in Jerusalem? If the birds became silent, and the creatures of the field herded together, as in some unwonted terror, what was the fear that fell upon men? What was the terror that fell upon the multitude who had cried out, "His blood be upon us, and upon our children"? (*Matt.* 27:25). They already saw the witness of God's wrath coming to take them at their word. Along the streets of Jerusalem men could not find their way; they encountered one another in the darkness; they fell flat on the earth for fear or sat on the doorsteps, not knowing where to find their home.

If there was fear in the streets of Jerusalem, what was there in the houses of Annas and of Caiaphas and of Pilate? What was there in the homes and in the hearts of those who had consciously shed the innocent blood? The darkness was also upon the Temple, and in the Holy of Holies; and the priests could not see to accomplish the sacrifice. The sacrifice was interrupted, and they could not see each other's face. The Sanctuary was filled with the tokens of the wrath of God and of the departure of His Presence. Such was the darkness which covered all the earth; and in the midst of it, and in a darkness—if possible, deeper than that which was visible—Jesus cried with a loud voice: "My God, My God, why hast Thou forsaken Me?"

Now, brethren, this is the part of our Lord's Passion to which I wish to draw your thoughts, and I wish to connect it with the profound truth on which our minds have been set in all the past days—I mean the sorrow for sin, the conversion of the soul, contrition of heart, the grace of compunction, by which we obtain pardon through the Most Precious Blood. But here is a wonder and a mystery. That God should become incarnate is in itself a mystery of faith; and yet, to God's omnipotence all things are possible. That God, being made man, should be tempted, seems to follow from the nature of His humanity—that being made man He should die is only the law of man, and He accepted it for our sakes; but that He should be forsaken of His Father, that His sinless soul should be darkened, that He should taste this penalty which is attached to guilt—this is indeed a mystery, this is a wonder which surpasses all beside. Let us, then, try to understand what was this dereliction, this isolation, this darkness, this solitude of the divine soul of Jesus—let us trace, as far as it is possible for us, what was its nature, what were its reasons, what are its instructions to us.

1. It consisted in three things; and the first of those three things was the unutterable and unconsoled and unrelieved pain of the body. When He was in His temptation, after He had fasted forty days and forty nights, angels came and ministered unto Him. He was refreshed in the faintness and in the exhaustion of His temptation. In the Agony of the Garden, when He sweat great drops of Blood, there was seen an angel from Heaven strengthening Him. Holy angels were

about Him in His temptation and in His Agony; but upon the Cross—not one. There was no ray of consolation, no ministering of relief; He hung upon the Cross with the whole weight of His Sacred Humanity, and with the unrelieved anguish of His frame. As He had said before: "Thinkest thou not that I cannot ask my Father, and he would send me twelve legions of angels?" (*Matt.* 26:53). If He had had the will to ask it, there would have been angelic ministries in myriads round about Him. He had not the will to ask it: He deprived Himself of their ministry and of their relief; and He seemed to plead with His Father, as much as to say, "Thou knowest My need, and yet I will not ask it. Thou knowest well My weakness and My pain, and Thou couldst relieve Me if Thou wouldst; and if in Thy wisdom Thou seest it good, I trust Myself in Thy hands—I will not ask Thee."

It is impossible, dear brethren, for any words of ours to draw out, or in the least to describe, the agony of the Crucifixion; and for myself, I always feel when attempts are made to picture or to paint the agonies of the Cross that they not only fall short of our thoughts, but they seem to deaden our feeling. How is it possible to understand the agony of those cold wounds from a whole night of scourging, the long hours in which His Sacred Flesh was furrowed to the bone? And now those wounds, grown cold in the chill of the night, were opened once more upon Calvary, when from His Sacred Body they rudely dragged His garments, all clotted with dried blood and cleaving to His wounds. Who can conceive this bodily anguish?

Who can imagine the crown of thorns with which He had been twice crowned—which had been beaten upon His head, and had been torn from His head in the stripping, and again forced upon His brows—that crown of thorns, which hindered all power of resting His head upon the Cross; for if it touched the Cross, the thorns pierced deeper? Or who can conceive the rending of those wounds when—the sharp nails driven through His hands and feet—the whole weight of His body stretched and tore them open till the very structure of the hands and feet was distorted? Or who can conceive the thirst— the parching, the drying thirst of that Sacred Body, which wrung from Him the cry, "I thirst"—that is, the dying of the whole frame when the vital spirits ebbed, the draining of blood, the chilling of the wind, the fulfillment to the letter of the words of the Psalmist in prophecy: "My tongue cleaveth to the roof of my mouth. Thou hast brought me into the dust of death"? (*Ps.* 21:16).

Dear brethren, I cannot attempt—and I feel you would rather I should not attempt, but that I should leave to your hearts—the conception of the bodily pains of our Divine Redeemer. And all this without relief. There was no ministry of so much as one angel to help Him; there was no diminution of one anguish of the body; but He suffered to the last all the agony of His Crucifixion; and in the midst of it His Heavenly Father left Him there, to drink of the chalice which He had chosen, even to the last drop, and all alone to die.

2. But next there was a desolation, if possible, deeper still. It was not only for the three hours that He hung upon the Cross, but for three-and-thirty years He had been the Man of Sorrows. There were two thieves, two malefactors, crucified with Him, one on the right and one on the left, and they suffered the same bodily agony; but He had another anguish of which they knew nothing—there was the unimaginable loneliness of the Son of God.

The sympathy of the Son of God is so large that He can feel with and for every son of man. There is not among the sons of men any so outcast, with whom the Son of God cannot sympathize in all the largeness of His Sacred Heart, and all the tenderness of His manhood. He knows all our sorrows, He knows all our sadness, He knows all the wounds of our hearts, He knows even the miseries we have brought upon ourselves by sin; and though sinless Himself, He is touched by the feeling of our infirmities, and has compassion on us. But for Him there was no commensurate sympathy. He was in this creation of His own making, and in the midst of His own creatures, without the sympathy of one who could adequately sympathize with Him.

At the most we are but creatures—even His Immaculate and Blessed Mother, she was but a creature; and the sympathy of that immaculate heart, though the largest of all, was not adequate to the great sorrow of the Son of God. All His friends, all His disciples, all His brethren, all that were round about Him, were incapable of meeting the demands for sympathy, such as the Sacred Heart of Jesus needed. This was the filling up of the divine loneliness of the Sacred Heart through all His earthly life—the completion of those three-and-thirty years of absolute and divine solitude. We think He was alone when He was in the desert in His temptation. He was indeed alone, but not more alone than when He was in the crowded streets of Jerusalem. The Sacred Heart of Jesus was too large, too divine, to find any companion, any fellow; and upon the Cross those mental sorrows were at their full. All the streams had run into the deep sea of that last sorrow, of which He said: "My soul is sorrowful even unto death."

"My soul!" The whole abyss of that human and

deified soul of the Son of God, with a capacity of sorrow beyond our imagination, was filled with sorrow—and even "unto death." What were those sorrows? First of all, for three-and-thirty years He had been in a world of sin, and in contact with sin. The Sinless One had breathed an atmosphere which is laden with our sins. He had looked upon countenances, of which every one bore the marks, and most of them the distortion, of sin. His ears had been filled with voices which had the sharpness of sin. Sin had come and breathed upon Him. Sin conversed with Him. Sin came and looked in His face. Sin came to Him, not knowing who it was; and the Holy One was surrounded—crowded upon by sinners. For three-and-thirty years He endured this agony; and the Agony in the Garden, when He sweat drops of blood, was but the last expression of that mental anguish which He had endured throughout all the long years of His earthly life.

He had not only lived in the midst of this atmosphere of evil, but He had been tempted. The tempter had drawn near to Him—the tempter, with insolence, had come to suggest evil to that divine and sinless Heart—to suggest to Him mistrust of His Heavenly Father, to suggest to Him presumption, to put before Him visions of ambition, of self-love, of vainglory. The anguish of that temptation can be known only to those that are sinless.

Besides this, for three-and-thirty years He had looked upon the vision of death—He, the Creator of all things, who knew the perfection of His own work, who knew to what pattern He had formed it, for what use and for what end—He saw it ruined and a wreck—trampled down, disfigured, dying daily. Lazarus in the tomb was a holy and beautiful example of that law of dissolution, compared with the universal death which

He saw devouring His creatures—the whole creation groaning and travailing in pain together.

Once more. He could not trust even His own friends. There was one whom He had called to be a disciple, chosen to be an Apostle, one whom He had taught with His divine words, whom He had impressed with the miracles of His power, whom He had commissioned to go out and preach His kingdom, whom He had fed at last with His Body and Blood, whose feet He washed in that last night of His sorrow; and even he, His own familiar friend—he sold Him; and having sold Him, he betrayed Him; and betraying Him, he betrayed Him with a kiss.

There was another sorrow—He was hated of men. Have you ever been hated by anybody? Do you know what it is to have the malice of someone who hates you pursuing you everywhere? Or have you ever known what it is to be hated by someone who never takes the pains or trouble to pursue you? Are you conscious that to be the object of hatred to anyone, justly or unjustly, is an exceeding bitterness, and a pain whenever we remember it? Now He was conscious at all times that He was an object of universal and preternatural hatred by the multitudes of Jerusalem. He knew that He had been condemned unjustly, accused falsely; that lying witness had been borne against Him, but that men believed Him to be guilty of the blasphemies of which He was accused. God knew His innocence, and a handful of His disciples, and the poor it may be, for they "heard him gladly" (*Mark* 12:37); but the rulers, and the rich, and the Pharisees, and the scribes, and the lawyers, and the chief priests, and those who were the leaders of the people, and the multitudes who were deceived by them, believed Him to be guilty. They hated Him for His guilt. And they hated Him for His holiness too; He was the object of hatred, not only because they had accused and condemned Him, but because His presence rebuked them; and to the Sacred Heart of Jesus, full of pity and compassion and tenderness and of pardon, giving His own life-blood for the salvation of His enemies, praying for them on the Cross, "Father, forgive them, for they know not what they do" (*Luke* 23:34), the consciousness of that hatred was an intensity of anguish.

But, perhaps He had friends still that were faithful. There were indeed, loving hearts—there was His Immaculate Mother, always near the Cross; there was the Beloved Disciple, who never forsook Him; there was poor Mary Magdalen, who stood with the spotless and sinless. Where were the rest? Where was Peter? He was somewhere with his head covered in his mantle, weeping bitterly. And where were the rest? Scattered afar off—not a friend near Him: even His own dearest friends had forsaken Him.

And then, lastly, there was the greatest sorrow of the Son of God—the consciousness that in that hour the great sin of the world had been accomplished: that man had laid hands upon God, that after thousands of years of sin and of rebellion, he had overtaken Him at last. The divine presence being out of the reach of man, God had become incarnate. At last God was made man—God came into the midst of men—God was within the reach of the arms of men; and they laid hands upon Him, they scourged Him, they blasphemed Him, and they put Him to death. The world murdered its own Maker, and sinners slew their own Redeemer. The world shed the Blood of God; it stained itself, and imprecated upon itself the Blood of the Divine Innocent.

He foresaw in that hour the multitude of souls that, notwithstanding the shedding of His Precious Blood, would never be saved—the redeemed souls, who shall go down alive into Hell—souls in multitudes who should never hear His name, and would yet sin against Him—souls in multitudes, still worse, who having heard His name would still sin against Him—souls on whom He had poured out the grace of His Holy Spirit, and who nevertheless would do despite to Him, and perish impenitent, and go down, like the leaves in autumn, countless in their multitude, into eternal death. All these sorrows, these mental sorrows, which in prophecy were before Him all His lifetime, rose at last to their fullness, and inundated the Sacred Heart in the hour of His Passion. But there is still one more part of this suffering. He might well say on the Cross, "My friends, My friends, why have you forsaken Me?" but His true desolation was this, that He had to cry, "My God, my God, why hast thou forsaken me?" (*Ps.* 21:2). That men forsake Me is no wonder—I know what is in man; but that Thou shouldst forsake Me? Why is it?

Now, brethren, we come to what I said in the beginning is a divine depth of mystery—round about which, indeed, we may walk in adoration; into which we shall never be able to descend—still there is somewhat of this mystery that we can understand. First of all, let us understand what that sorrow was not. It was not a separation of the Son from the Father. The Father and the Son and the Holy Ghost are one God—consubstantial, the Uncreated, the Infinite, the Ever-Blessed; therefore it was nothing whatsoever of separation of the Son from the Father, or of the Father from the Son. Again: the Godhead and the Humanity in the One Person of Jesus Christ, from the moment of the Incarnation, by hy-

postatic union—that is, by union in one person—are in-
dissolubly united to all eternity; and therefore those
words did not import or imply a shadow of separation
between the Godhead and the Manhood of Jesus
Christ.

What, then, do they signify? Just as, in the Agony in
the Garden, the light and the sweetness and the consolation of His Godhead were voluntarily withdrawn
from the suffering of His Manhood, because He had
chosen for our sakes to let in the full tide and flood of
sorrow to fill His Sacred Heart, so upon the Cross. We
know what follows after our sins—what darkness and
desolation come upon us; but this comes from our corruption, from our rebellion, from the sin that is in us.
The Son of God, the Holy One, had our humanity; but
in that humanity there was no disorder, no corruption,
no spot of sin, for He had deified our humanity; and
therefore all that He suffered was by a voluntary act of
His own—willingly withdrawing for a time the sweetness and the light and the consolation of His Heavenly
Father. From the first moment of the Incarnation, as
you know, the human soul of Jesus was in the beatific
vision: with His human soul Jesus saw God; He loved
God with His whole heart, and He worshipped God
with His whole soul; and while He was on earth a
wayfarer, He was already in the possession and fruition
of the beatific vision.

But in the Agony in the Garden and in the three
hours upon the Cross He voluntarily withdrew, as it
were, the light and the sweetness which He always had
by right as God, and by merit as Man. He allowed a
veil, a cloud—as the darkness covered the sun at that
hour—to spread over His soul. He allowed a darkness
to be drawn between the sweetness and the light of His

Godhead and His human soul; and why was this? It was for our sakes. It was as voluntary as His Incarnation, as His Temptation, as His Agony, as His Death; He was offered up, because He willed it; He was troubled in the Garden, because He willed it; He was desolate upon the Cross, because He willed it. It was His own voluntary act, and that for our sakes.

It was not only voluntary; it was also vicarious—it was suffered in our stead. And why? Because the penalty of our sin is separation from God; because separation from God is eternal death. Because the loss of God is Hell; because the penalty of sin is the loss of God. Because, even after death, those who are saved, unless their sins be perfectly expiated, will be detained from the vision of God; because in this life every sin we commit is followed by a shadow; and that shadow is darkness, and that darkness is a part of desolation. And because we are under this law, holy, just, and good, by which every sin is followed by the penalty of desolation, He who, to expiate all our sins and pains, voluntarily and vicariously suffered all that His sinless and Divine Soul could suffer, permitted Himself, in that moment of His agony, to be deprived of the sweetness and consolation and light even of His own Godhead. The inferior part of His Humanity, which suffered like as ours, was in the dust of death, in the sorrows of this world, and in the desolation of the hiding of His Father's face.

And now, why was this? First, as I have said, to make expiation. It was to expiate our sin and our pains, to save us from that and from worse. He endured it for our sakes; and He endured it that He might reveal His love. He had revealed His love by every manifestation, by works of mercy, by healing lepers, by giving sight to the blind, by raising the dead, by absolving the penitent. He had spoken words of grace such as never came out of the lips of man—words which were more than the words of man; and if men had had hearts to understand, they would have known them to be words of a Divine Person; but these things were not enough: they did not even yet persuade us of the great mystery of His love. He had need of another language, of other words, of something more articulate, something more convincing, something more persuasive: and what could that be?

Sorrow unto death, penalty even to the extreme verge of what is possible for the Son of God to suffer; and therefore He chose, voluntarily and vicariously, to endure all things that His Divine Soul could endure for our sakes, to convince us, if possible, of His love—if possible, to make us believe how much He loves us—if possible, to prevail over the hardness of our hearts, that we at last may be convinced and persuaded of the exceeding love of our Divine Redeemer, and all this to make us trust His love, that by love He may win our love again. He knew that it is not by command that we can be made to love Him, it is not by reasoning that the love of God is awakened in the heart, it is not by any means whatsoever save only by the manifestation of love. As we know among ourselves, it is love that awakens love, it is friendship that kindles friendship, it is the sensible manifestation of kindness and of tenderness of heart, of disinterested and self-denying love—it is this that awakens us to love again; so is it towards Him. And He therefore endured all things first, to persuade us to trust in His love.

The great sin of the world is that it does not trust in the love of God. It is your great sin. It is the cause of all your sins. You never could sin against God if you had the feeling of His love to you; you never could venture, you could not endure to do it. If you felt the love of God to you personally, as you feel the warmth of the noonday sun, it would be impossible with the knowledge of your heart to sin against Him. It would be morally impossible. It would be the violation of your new nature. He said: "Greater love hath no man than this: if a man give his life for his friends." (*John* 15:13). He has given His life for you. What can He say to you, what could He do for you, if this will not persuade you? Is it in the power of the Word of God to convince you of the love of Jesus Christ, if His agony on the Cross is not enough? Therefore, He is all day long saying these words to you: "O My friends, it was for you I was crucified. O My Beloved, it is you I have loved even unto death. O My children, for you I shed My Precious Blood. What more could I have done for you than that which I have done? What more could I have given than that which I have given? What more could I suffer for you than that which I have already suffered? But you will not come unto Me that you may have life—you will not believe My love. How often would I have gathered you under the shadow of My Cross! How often would I have covered you with the hem of My garment! For I have sought after you, to try and bring you within My own Sacred Heart; but ye would not."

He has been burning with love to us, and we have stood at a distance, cold and unmoved. He says to us from the Cross: "What more could I do? What more could I give? What more could I suffer? If there were anything I could suffer, I would suffer it still. If it were necessary to die again for you to save you, I would die again. If it were possible to suffer more, it should be suffered." And what is your answer? I do not mean in words, I mean in deeds. He says to us: "I have loved you not in word, but in deed. I have loved you not in professions, but in Passion and Death. I have loved you not in such protestations as Peter made to Me, but by a reality which no man can deny, no man can fail to understand. I suffered death upon the Cross for you. I was forsaken even of My Father; and that for your sakes."

Here, then, dear brethren, we have the meaning in some little measure, the mere outline of this dereliction of our Divine Lord. It consisted in the unrevealed agonies of the body, in the unconsoled sorrows of His Sacred Heart; and lastly, in that mysterious taste of darkness and desolation, in the withdrawal of the light and the sweetness of the countenance of God, even in the hour of His death.

Now, why was this? When we are in sorrow and in trouble of mind; when pains of body, sharp sicknesses, unkindness, ingratitude, the forsaking of friends, the bitterness of life; when dryness of heart, darkness of soul—when these things come upon us, we have no need to say, "My God, my God, why hast Thou forsaken me?" We know why, or we might know, and we ought to know in one moment. It is no mystery why we should be forsaken. Look back on your mortal sins in childhood and boyhood, and youth and manhood, and the mortal sins that you remember, and the mortal sins you have forgotten, and the mortal sins that you have not repented as you ought even to this day. We have no reason to ask, "Why hast Thou forsaken me?" Look back upon the cloud of venial sins, which through long years you have been committing—sins of self-love, sins of vanity, sins of sloth, sins of ingratitude, sins of neglect of God, sins of hardness of heart with the crucifix before your eyes, sins of voluntary coldness even in the presence of the Blessed Sacrament—look at that cloud of venial sins which you commit, perhaps every day of your lives. We have no need to ask, "Why hast Thou forsaken me?"

Once more. The sins of omission that you commit, the duties that you so readily leave undone, the acts of love and fidelity to our Divine Master which with such lukewarmness you offer to Him, the great want of generosity in all your life, the want of love responding to His love, and tenderness to His tenderness—surely these things explain why our hearts should be cold and dark, and our prayers dry, and why we should be buffeted with temptation, and why we should find no solace. We have no difficulty in understanding this. Nay, more—look at our instabilities. What a life is ours! We serve God by fits and by starts; we have cold fits and hot fits, like men in an ague, like those that are struck by fever—sometimes we are in earnest, sometimes we give up; we are carried away by gusts of temptation; a frown of the world will kill off all our good resolutions. Such is our life, perpetually tossed to and fro, like waves of the sea. Where is our stability? And if we are unstable, why is it? Because we do not love. A friend that loves a friend does not vary in his friendship. The variations of friendship show how shallow and how reckless our love is.

And lastly, I say reckless; and by reckless I mean this—that we live all the day long as if Christ had never died for us. Dear brethren, ask yourselves what one thing is there that you left undone yesterday for the recollection of the Passion of Jesus Christ—for I hope

you were then remembering the day of His Agony in
the Garden. You remember that we were yesterday on
the eve of the day of His Crucifixion. We are in Holy
Week and in the midst of the thoughts of the Passion of
Jesus Christ. Is it the chief thought in your hearts?
What did all this do for you yesterday, or what one
thing did you do or leave undone for the love of our
Lord in His Passion? And if this be so, we have no
reason to wonder that we have sorrows, pains, chastisements, rods, visitations, desolations. We lose the light
of our Father's countenance. The sweetness and the
consolation which we had once, it may be, are gone.
We have them no longer; but the fault is our own.

Well, now let us learn for what end and purpose this
is. If Jesus Christ did not love us, He would leave us to
sin and to prosper, He would leave us to go on as we
are, and to enjoy the world. These are the words of
God: "Whom the Lord loveth he chastiseth; and
scourgeth every son whom he receiveth." (*Prov.* 3:12;
Heb. 12:6). If you be without chastisement, whereof all
are partakers, then are you no true sons of God. The
sign and the token of the love of our Divine Lord is
when He takes the thorns of His Crown and puts them
into our head, and the nails of His Crucifixion and runs
them into our hands and feet; the feet which we have
used to do evil and to walk in ways contrary to His will,
them He crucifies; and the hands that have been busy
in vanity and folly and worldliness, and worse—on
them in His love He will imprint the marks of His own
Crucifixion; and upon the heart that has been un-
faithful to Him, that has been wandering, selfish, care-
less, self-indulgent, He impresses the tokens of His Passion.

By crosses, sicknesses, visitations, bereavements,

afflictions, chastisements, and rods—by those sacred spiritual visitations of desolation and of dryness—by these He wakens us up to know Him; to see that we are offending against Him, and that the penal consequences of our sins and faults have found us out. He permits them to come upon us, and permits them in pity for our sanctification. He knows that without them we cannot be saved; He knows that without them we should sin and prosper, that we should go on in our worldly way, and should never see God; and therefore He uses these things with a manifold wisdom, with an exceeding tenderness. He uses them first to check us, and if need be, to strike us down.

A sinner in the guilt of his sin is struck down sometimes like Saul on the way to Damascus. A light from Heaven which no eye but his can see, and he alone can recognize, strikes him down with the consciousness of himself, so that when he rises up he is blind to the world, and his eyes are opened upon his own state, his own peril, and his own guilt. It is in times of affliction, sorrow, sickness, anxiety, and pain of heart and mind— and in these last above all—that this loving stroke of our Divine Saviour's hand is felt. He sends or permits these desolations and sorrows to chastise us, to make us recollect what it is we have done. I dare say you all know what it is to feel sad and cast down, and to say: "I do not know why it is—I know there is some cause; and I know I felt it, and knew it at the moment; but I cannot remember now what it is that has brought me this sadness." After a little pause of thought, we trace out the real reason—we remember what it was; we have found how justly He has dealt with us; and this chastisement gives us a self-knowledge, without which there is little contrition. Moreover, it is by these trials that He puts to test the love that we profess to Him.

It is a poor love which is warm only in the sunshine. It is a mean love of God which does not burn even under a cross. If we only serve God because it is sweet—if we only turn from sin because we are afraid of Hell—if our motives for doing right, are that we have a servile fear of doing wrong, we are mercenaries and hirelings, we are unworthy of the pure and generous love of Jesus Christ. He, the sinless Son of God, endured all things for us—not for His own sake, but solely and purely for ours; and we serve Him only for our own. It is by these penal consequences of our sins that He tests our love and purifies it, that He cleanses it of self-love, self-indulgence, and of all that dwelling upon self, of wounded self, of that pity for ourselves, springing from the self-love of our heart which towards God is—I will not say dead, but that it has little pulse and little warmth within it.

Lastly, whatever sorrows you have of the body, of the mind, or of the soul, these are intended to produce in you one thing above all—that is, compunction. Compunction means sorrow for sin, springing from the love of the Five Sacred Wounds which Jesus suffered in our behalf. Attrition, as you know, means the sorrow of the heart that is bruised; contrition, the sorrow of the heart that is broken; compunction, the sorrow of the heart that is pierced with Jesus Christ. Until we have come to the foot of the Cross, and have contemplated the Five Wounds of our Divine Saviour, and the love of the Sacred Heart through His side opened by the lance, and until we have entered into His love, and sorrowed because of that love, and because of our own want of love, and because of our own ingratitude, our sorrow is not worthy of the name of compunction.

He is perfecting in you this generous sorrow. If you are suffering pains of body, unite them with the sufferings of Jesus Christ upon His Cross. If you have mental pains, sorrows of mind, trials of your family, ingratitude of friends, disobedience of children, the loss of those dear to you, whatsoever it be, unite them with the mental sorrows of Jesus dying upon the Cross. If you are suffering spiritual dryness and darkness, and desolation and distance from God, as you think, unite them with His Dereliction. Do not say, "My God, my God, why hast Thou forsaken me?" Say, "My God, my God, I know well how I deserve this desolation. I know well how all my life has merited that I should be forsaken; but my hope is in Thy love, which has never forsaken those that trust in Thee."

Therefore, dear brethren, sum up all I have said, and sum it up in these two ways: first of all, choose of your own will, gladly and willingly, a lot of sorrow and of the Cross in this world, rather than a lot that is bright and fair. If they were both before you, held out in the hands of our Divine Saviour, the one the lot of His Cross, the other the happiness of this world, remember what was set before Him in the mountain: "All these things will I give thee, if thou falling down wilt adore me." (*Matt.* 4:9). Put the world aside—we cannot serve two masters—it is better to choose the lot that He chose for Himself; to be made like to Him even in His Cross. It is safer for us, because it is more generous towards Him. Next, if we have not the heart and courage to choose this for His sake, let us bless Him, if, contrary to our will, He choose it for us. If He sends us this very lot from which we shrink, then let us bless the wise and loving Physician, who, seeing that we are cowardly— that we have neither nerve nor firmness to take the knife to lay the wound open, and that the wound if it fester will bring death—let us bless Him that He in His love and tenderness has chosen the lot of the Cross for us, has given it to us, and that we have no choice to make but to accept it, to press it to our heart, to love it for His sake, and to pray to Him to give us grace to bear it.

We have offended against Him by every member of the body, by every faculty of the mind, by every passion of the heart, by every affection of the soul; and upon the Cross in His bodily pain, and in His mental sorrow, and in His spiritual desolation, He made a perfect and complete expiation for all our sins. They are all expiated; and in His Precious Blood they will all be washed away on one condition—that we are made like to Him; and if we can be made like to Him only by being crucified, then let us be crucified.[1] A will at variance with His will is sin and eternal death; a will crucified with His will is holiness and eternal life.

Let us pray Him, then, to do His own work in us; let us say to Him, "Lord, Thou wast crucified for me, crucify me with Thyself. I cannot save myself; Thou only canst save me—save me, lest I perish eternally." Pray Him to crucify the living will which is within you, for "they that are Christ's have crucified the flesh, with the affections and concupiscences." This is the token of a Christian. Pray Him to do it until you can say these three words: "God forbid I should glory, save in the cross of our Lord Jesus Christ, whereby the world is crucified unto me and I unto the world." (*Gal.* 6:14). And again: "With Christ I am nailed to the Cross, nevertheless I live; yet not I, but Christ liveth in me; and the life that I now live in the flesh, I live by faith in the Son of God, who loved me and delivered himself to death for me." (*Gal.* 2:19-20). Let us say to Him every day: "Lord, whether I live let me live unto thee, and whether I die, let me die unto thee, that living and dying I may be thine." (*Rom.* 14:8).

NOTES

1. Thus Our Lord's expiation of our sins is assimilated to our souls through contrition, Confession, amendment of life and the doing of penance—these acts being efficacious through the life-giving grace of Jesus Christ.

Sermon VIII

THE JOYS OF THE RESURRECTION

"Jesus said unto her: Mary. She saith unto him: Rabboni; that is to say, Master."

—John 20:16

It was very early in the morning, while it was yet dark, that Mary Magdalen and the other women came to the garden; and they found the stone rolled away from the mouth of the sepulcher. Mary Magdalen ran and told Peter and the Disciple whom Jesus loved, saying: "They have taken away the Lord out of the sepulcher, and we know not where they have laid Him." Peter and John ran to the garden; John outran Peter, and came first to the sepulcher, and stooping down looked in; but Peter following, came, and went into the sepulcher, and saw the linen clothes lying. Then they returned to their home; but Mary Magdalen lingered. She had no home but the sepulcher of Jesus. It was empty, but she would not go away. She stood without weeping: and as she wept she stooped down and looked into the sepulcher, and saw two angels in white—the one sitting at the head, and the other at the feet, where the Body of Jesus had lain. Jesus stood behind her, and said to her: Woman, why weepest thou? Whom seekest thou? And she, turning and seeing Him, but believing that He was the gardener, saith: "They have taken my Lord out of the sepulcher, and we know not where they have laid Him. Sir, if thou hast taken Him away, tell me where I may find Him, that I may take Him away." And Jesus saith unto her: "Mary!" She saith unto Him: "Rabboni!" that is to say, Master. She had lingered out of love and compunction; she knew that she had pierced her Lord by her sins and for her sins; and she stood weeping at the sepulcher; and her lingering was rewarded. She was rewarded with the vision of angels—she was rewarded with the vision of Jesus Himself.

Now, dear brethren, we have here revealed to us the law and the order of the joy and consolation of the Kingdom of God. They that suffer and sorrow most shall be the most consoled and fullest of joy in His Kingdom. He who suffered most and sorrowed most was the Man of Sorrows, who for our sakes was crucified. He said before His agony: "My soul is sorrowful even unto death." (*Matt.* 26:38). The deified Soul of Jesus—a Soul like ours, because He was a man; a Soul unlike ours, because It was deified by union with the Godhead—had a capacity for sorrow that no other human heart could ever know. As the sorrows of the Son of God Incarnate were the greatest that son of man ever tasted, so, in a measure according to the capacity of His Heart for sorrow, was the capacity of His Sacred Heart for joy. In the hour of His Resurrection, He was filled with the joy of His Kingdom, and rejoiced over His accomplished work, over the redemption of the world, over the sevenfold shedding of His Precious Blood, over the remission of our sins, over the vision of grace and the multitude of His elect who should be saved eternally. Jesus in that hour rejoiced with a heart filled with a divine joy, which we may adore, but cannot comprehend.

Next after His was the joy of His Immaculate Mother, the Mother of Seven Sorrows; and as each sorrow was sevenfold, so was her joy likewise a sevenfold joy. Though, dear brethren, we do not read it in the text of the Holy Gospels—for many things are not written which Jesus did, the which if they should all be written, the world itself would not contain the books—the Church has believed always, by the light and intuition of faith, that the first to whom He manifested Himself in the glory of His Resurrection was His blessed and sinless Mother, who, next to the Man of Sorrows, suffered more deeply and more sharply than any human heart. And next after the Mother of God, to whom did He show Himself in His joy? Was it to Peter, whom He had made the Rock of His imperishable Church? Was it to John, who had lain upon His bosom at supper?

It was to Mary Magdalen, out of whom He had cast seven devils, from whose soul He had washed away in the Precious Blood sins sevenfold, red as scarlet, beyond all number—to her, because she had loved much, and because out of her great love she sorrowed much; and because next after the Mother of God herself—her sorrows were the greatest—He first showed Himself in the glory of His Resurrection. He came and stood behind her, while she was weeping at the sepulcher; and, while she did not recognize Him, He called her by her name. He called her by the name so familiar; He said unto her, "Mary!" and the accent of His well-known voice revealed to her who it was. She answered Him as she was wont to answer, "Rabboni!" that is to say, Master. And after her, next He manifested Himself to Peter—the unstable, faithless friend, who had three times denied Him; and after Peter to His Disciples, faithful, fearful souls, true to Him still, though their hearts could not endure the perils of His Crucifixion.

Here, then, we have laid open to us a great law of the Kingdom of God, namely, that the joy of the Resurrection is measured out according to the sorrow of our penitence, according to the sorrow that we have endured here in the body, in the mind, and in the soul. As we have tasted of His Cross and of His desolation, so in the Kingdom of the Resurrection we shall taste of His glory and of His joy; and these forty days on which we have just entered are, as it were, the type and the shadow, and the foretaste and the beginning of this eternal joy. Those forty days, when Jesus was always near them, but not always seen—always, as it were, ready to manifest Himself, and yet still hiding Himself—those days in which they first knew the fullness of His Godhead, were indeed days of surpassing joy, as of Heaven upon earth; and yet not heavenly alone, but earthly too, that is, He came down to them in their sorrows and their humiliations. He did not ascend at once to the throne of His glory; but as by the Incarnation He had humbled Himself to be made man and to enter within the sphere of our sympathies, so in those forty days, when He had revealed His Godhead, He came to tarry in the midst of them, to speak with them, to eat and drink with them, to suffer them to touch Him. If He forbade Mary Magdalen in the first moment of her joy, yet He suffered Thomas to handle the wounds of His hands and side; and therefore those forty days bring before us both the joys of faith, and the joys of vision. By the Resurrection of our Lord the fountains of the great deep of the joy in Heaven were broken up, and the whole Church, according to the prophecy, was inundated by the river which makes glad the City of God.

The Church of God is inundated to this day by this torrent of sweetness. Notwithstanding the warfare of the Church upon earth, notwithstanding the bitter and relentless persecutions of the world, notwithstanding the Cross, which we must all bear, one by one, if we are true disciples of our Master; nevertheless, there is a joy which He has given and no man can take from us—a joy so inward, so deep, so expanding, so multiplying as life goes on, that it is a foretaste of our eternal joy.

1. First, there are the joys of faith. In what do they consist? In the same in which the joy of the Disciples consisted in the forty days, that is, in the presence of Jesus. He ascended to His Father; but He is with us still. To go to His Father is not to be absent from us; it is, indeed, to be out of sight, but He is always near; and therefore the Apostle said to the Christians at Philippi, "Rejoice in the Lord always; and again I say rejoice. Let your modesty," your moderation, "be known unto all men" (*Phil.* 4:4-5); that is, your self-control, your self-command, your Christian dignity; for "the Lord is nigh," you are always in His presence. He is indeed "at the right hand of the Father," according to the natural mode of His existence; but He showed Himself to Stephen in the moment of his martyrdom; He showed Himself to Saul on the way to Damascus, He stood by him in his answer before the imperial tribunal in Rome; He has manifested Himself to saints again and again; He is with us always; and He will come again. We know that He will be seen once more upon earth; and between His first appearance and His last, though withdrawn from our ordinary sight, He is still near to us. We know that we are in His presence, and the joy of His presence is our joy; but there is another Presence, perpetual, universal, intimate, veiled indeed, but real

and personal, always upon the altar. Wheresoever the Holy Catholic Church is, there is Jesus, reigning in the mystery of the Blessed Sacrament, always near to us; and our union with Him is a union so intimate that the mind cannot define it; the heart alone, illuminated by faith, can know by consciousness that which the intellect cannot comprehend.

But not only is His presence the source of our joy, but also our loosing from sin and death, which is now at this moment true and real, and if we be faithful shall be eternal. We know that the Sacrament of Holy Baptism was instituted by our Divine Saviour to raise the soul by a spiritual resurrection from the death of Original Sin. It is a matter of revelation, and therefore a matter of faith and of the divine certainty of faith, that those who are baptized are born again, made children of God, receive the gift of supernatural life, are loosed from the bond of Original Sin, and therefore from the doom of eternal death. Dear brethren, this has passed upon you all. You were every one of you baptized in the unconsciousness of infancy. While as yet your will had never varied or opposed itself to the will of our Redeemer, you received the grace of your regeneration—you were loosed from sin and death. If you have fallen under its dominion again—if you have willfully become sinful, you have indeed been again condemned to die; but if you have preserved the grace of your Baptism, you are now loosed from sin and death, the power of the Resurrection is upon you. If since your Baptism you have fallen again into mortal sin and so have died once more, there is another Sacrament instituted in the Precious Blood, the Sacrament of Penance; and it is a matter of divine revelation and of divine faith, that all who with true contrition receive the absolution of that

Sacrament are once more loosed from all their actual sins, and therefore from eternal death.

Here, then, is the first source of our joy. Why, then, is it we do not rejoice? Because our hearts are cold, and our faith is dim. These great realities are like the presence of God round about us, in the midst of which we walk to and fro every day unconsciously. And once more: if we have faith, and if we lay to heart the truths that I have tried to speak, then we have the consciousness in us of a risen life. As there is a soul which quickens the body, so there is a supernatural life which quickens the soul; and we know that as we have the power of the body, so, we have the power of the soul; and as thought, and intelligence, and motion descend from the head of the body into all our members, so the life that we now live, we live in virtue of our union with our Divine Head in Heaven. This is what the Apostle declares when he says: "There is therefore now no condemnation to those that are in Christ Jesus, who walk not according to the flesh, but according to the spirit. The law of the spirit of life in Christ Jesus hath made me free from the law of sin and death." (*Rom.* 8:1-2).

The spirit of the Resurrection, and the risen life of our Divine Head, are in every one of us, if we are not under the power of mortal sin; and we have this countersign, that if we are become new creatures, the "old things are passed away, all things have become new": that is to say, our old character, our old mind, our old habits, our old loves, our old hates, our old thoughts, our old sins, are stripped from us like a leprous garment. There they are, our grave clothes cast away; there they are, before us still, a vision of sin and death, reminding us of what we were once; but they are ourselves no longer. The spirit of life in us has sloughed them off, like the corrupt flesh of the leper. The wind-ing sheet and the bands of mortality in which we were when we were bound in sin, have been loosened and taken off; the old character is gone. If we are disciples of Jesus Christ, a new mind, new loves, new hatreds, new fears, new hopes, new aspirations, new affections, new desires, have sprung up in us. "If any man be in Christ Jesus, he is a new creature" (*2 Cor.* 5:17) and in a new creation. A change has passed upon him so great that he may feel day after day the words of our Divine Lord fulfilled in him: "In that day ye shall know that I am in my Father, and you in me, and I in you." (*John* 14:20).

2. In this we see an outline of the joys of faith, but we cannot longer dwell on them, for there are greater things than these. If these be the joys of faith, what are the joys of vision? What the ripeness of summer is after the bitter piercing cold and death of winter, such is the vision of God when the vision of faith shall melt into the glory of His Kingdom. The same truths, the same realities, the same persons, the same relations, which are here, will be there, and will be eternal. Like as when the snow melts away before the returning sun, the forms of nature, the very same as they were before they were buried, reappear; so shall it be in the vision of glory. This is the office and work of the Holy Ghost. Say the last words of your baptismal creed: "I believe in the Holy Ghost, in the Holy Catholic Church." The Church is His creation: One, because He is One; holy, because He is holy; infallible, because He is the Light of truth: "And in the communion of saints"—which is the ripe fruit gathered from the Church on earth into the garners of the Kingdom: "And in the forgiveness of sins"—in Baptism, in Penance, in contrition: "And in

the resurrection of the body," which shall be raised by the Holy Ghost from the dust, and knit together once more in its perfect glory: "And in life everlasting," which is the indwelling of the Holy Ghost in the souls of the blessed.

This, then, is the joy of vision. And what will be the first object of our sight? Our Divine Lord has said: "I am the door, by which if any man shall enter in, he shall be saved; and he shall go in and go out, and shall find pasture" (*John* 10:9)—that is, the pastures of eternal life. The presence of the Sacred Humanity of Jesus, the vision of our Divine Master in the glory of His Kingdom, is the fulfillment of the promise and the prophecy, "his eyes shall behold the king in his beauty, in the land that is far off." (*Is.* 33:17). And what is the beauty of the Son of God? The beauty of God Himself. He is the Brightness of His Father's Glory, the Image of His Substance; and God Himself is beauty. That Divine beauty was clothed in the human beauty. The first Adam was beautiful, for he was made unto the likeness and image of God, who is beauty itself; and he was made to the likeness and image of the Second Adam, that is, the Word Incarnate. And the very Person of Jesus Christ is, as the Word of God says, "the fairest among the children of men." (*Ps.* 44:3).

But this outward beauty, what is it compared with the inward beauty—with the love, and the pity, and the compassion, and the mercy, and the purity, and the sanctity of the Sacred Heart? We shall see the countenance of the Friend who has loved us, sorrowed for us, died for us; the countenance of the Son of God fixed upon each one of us; the eyes of our Redeemer looking upon us personally one by one; His voice speaking to us as He spoke to Mary at the sepulcher, calling us each one by name, knowing each one of us in all the intimate consciousness of our personality: this is the beginning of the joy.

And next the consciousness that, through the whole realm of His Kingdom there is but one Will, holy, supreme, and sovereign; and that His will pervades our whole being, so that there is not a beat in the pulse, nor a motion of our whole spiritual nature, that is not in perfect harmony with His; and that the same Will pervades all that are about Him in all the heavenly court; all the holy Angels, all the companies of the Blessed; thereby creating one joy in all, and a mutual joy, so that the joy of all is the joy of each. We all shall have a perfect consciousness of our past in this world, a perfect personal identity, the same there as we were here— sin only excepted, a perfect recognition of each other, a perfect interchange of intuition and of mutual intelligence, of all that is in the soul, of each other's bliss and joy. The greatest in the kingdom of God—because their capacity is greater—shall have a greater joy in the glory of the least, and the least, because their charity is perfect, will rejoice with a greater joy in the glory of those that are higher in bliss than they.

Add to this that which would make even this earth blissful. If for one moment the conflicts, the hatreds, the contentions, the jealousies, the warfares, the jangling, the discords of this world could be suspended—if for one day from sunrise to sunset sin could cease, even this world would be blissful. In that world there shall be rest eternal; rest, that is, no temptation, warfare, or cross; rest within, heart, mind, soul, thought, affection, will—all in perfect harmony with the perfect will of Jesus. And—that which you perhaps will little realize when I say it—rest from toil, rest from labor, rest from eating bread in the sweat of your face—that which the multitudes and the millions of Christendom, in all lands and all languages, have for their earthly lot—the poor laborer, the tiller of the ground—those who wring hard sustenance out of the hard earth, who live lives of cold, and pain, and disease, and privation, in homes that are bare, with hungry children, with those that are dearest to them languishing, and fading for want of the food which their toil cannot supply—this is an earthly burden of which you who hear me perhaps know little. But in Heaven "they shall hunger no more, they shall thirst no more, neither shall the sun light upon them nor any heat; but the Lamb which is in the midst of the throne shall rule over them, and shall lead them by the fountains of the waters of life, and God shall wipe away all tears from their eyes." (*Apoc.* 7:16-17).

And once more: there shall be the joy of conscious eternal health. You have known perhaps in yourselves what pain and sickness is; what it is to languish long upon a bed of suffering; you remember the first day when you rose up again, and went out into the free air and into the light of the sun; when you felt that health had come back, and strength had returned to you, and that vigor was once more in your limbs: what, then, shall be the eternal health of the Kingdom of God, when there shall be no more death, no more disease, no more wasting of the poor body, no more crippled limbs, no more blind eyes, no more ears without hearing, no more distorted members, no more distracted minds, no more unsound brain, or wandering intelligence, or blankness of idiocy. These things shall be gone forever; for with the resurrection of the body they shall be healed eternally—and the soul being made perfect, after the image of Jesus, shall be clothed in a glorified

body like His own. As there is no more death, there
will be no more change. If in this world we had all the
desires of our hearts, they could not last forever; and if
they could last forever, they could not satisfy our
hearts; but in the Kingdom of God there shall be no
more change to all eternity. There shall be no yesterday, and there shall be no tomorrow, and there shall be
no sunset; it shall be one eternal day—now, ever-pre-
sent—the noon of overpassing bliss. The happiness of
life, the happiness of home, the happiness of your
past—where is it? You have to look back for it; it is
gone, or it is going, transient and fleeting, and in a little
while it will be no longer; but in the Kingdom of God,
that life ever new of body, of mind, of soul, of home, of
happiness, of perfect identity, of mutual recognition, of
restored bonds of love perfected and transfigured in the
kingdom of the Resurrection, shall all be changeless
and eternal.

There yet remains another joy; but it is one of which
I can hardly speak, because I can hardly understand.
We shall see God. We shall see Him as He is; our eyes
shall behold the Eternal. We shall see His uncreated
nature; we shall see that which our hearts cannot conceive; we shall see Him, not by the eyes of flesh and
blood, nor by the bare intellect of nature; but by the
Light of Glory. The Light of Glory is from the Holy
Ghost, the illumination of the intellect by the power of
the Holy Ghost. The soul filled with Charity will be
elevated by the Holy Ghost to the vision of God, and to
the union of all its powers and all its affections with the
uncreated Truth and the uncreated Love—that is, God
Himself. We shall see Him not in His infinity—for the
finite mind cannot—but we shall see Him fully.

Just as when we see a spark of fire we see all fire,

though the fire has no limit that we can understand; and
as when we see a ray of light we see the whole nature of
light, though that light be boundless; so we shall see
God. When we shall see His sanctity, purity, wisdom,
goodness, power, justice, mercy, pity, compassion, and
all the perfections of God, we shall see God as He is,
though not His infinity. And we shall see God the
Father in His uncreated essence; we shall see God the
Son begotten of the Father; we shall see God the Holy
Ghost proceeding from the Father and the Son; we shall
see the essence of the glory and of the eternal mutual
knowledge and of the eternal mutual love of the Three
co-equal Persons in One Godhead. These things sur-
pass both our words and our thoughts; but in the
Kingdom of the Resurrection they shall be manifested
to all who enter by that Door, which is Jesus Christ, by
whose light all shall be revealed. Here, then, are the
joys of the Resurrection.

And now, what are the notes, what are the marks of
those who are the heirs of that joy? You, as I have said,
by your Baptism have been made partakers of the
Resurrection; by your absolution you have been loosed
from sin and death; you are heirs therefore of the joys
of faith and of the joys of vision; but as the Church itself has its notes, so those that are the true disciples of
Jesus Christ have their visible notes, which are certain
fruits of the Holy Ghost; and what are they?

1. The first note, without which they are disciples
only in name, is this: the love of God and their neighbor. St. John says, speaking by the Holy Ghost, "We
know that we have passed from death unto life, because
we love the brethren. He that loveth not his brother
abideth in death." (*1 John* 3:14). The mark of a soul
that has the life of the Resurrection in it, is the love of

God above all things; the love of our neighbor as ourselves. The love of God above all things is the love of appreciation, so that we shall be willing to give up the whole world rather than lose God. The love of our neighbor is the warmth of charity sensibly felt by all around us. "Charity begins at home" means this: that there is no charity in the man who does not first pervade his own home with the love of God and his neighbor; and next, that love reaches our friends, each of them in their own order; and after our friends our enemies, and all who stand in need of us. And they who stand in need of us are the mourners, the outcast, the sick, the tempted, the lost, the little children who have no helpers, and lastly, our enemies, and those who bear us ill-will without a cause. If you desire to have a test whereby to know whether you have the life of the Resurrection in you, see how you bear yourselves to those whom you believe to bear ill-will to you. They are among your best friends. The friends that love you and speak fair and soft things to you are not friends, compared to those who look upon you with sharp eyes, and speak with cold voices, and bear unkind hearts. They try what you are; they try your patience, the spirit of your humility, whether you have a crucified will, which is the sure mark of the true disciple of Jesus Christ.

If you have enemies, look to see all that is good in them. There is good in them all. Just as when we look into thick tangled forests there are rays of the sun's light which come down on the leaves and on the earth, here and there, broken and scattered—little, it may be, but still the sun is there—so in the worst of men, unless they be reprobate, there are still some traces of God. Look and find them: if you have charity, you will have

eyes to see that sun's light; and though you cannot be
blind to their sin—for you must see it, if you have light
and discernment from the Holy Ghost—nevertheless, in
your conduct towards those who are sinful, and in your
treatment of sinners, you will be as if you were blind,
you will be even as our Lord is to you, who, although
He sees every sin in you, bears with you with an immutable patience—never sharpens His voice, never
makes a gesture of impatience, but seeing that the flax
is not yet quenched and the reed not yet broken, He
bears with you with a divine pity. So bear with your
enemies. And this charity of our hearts will overflow to
all the works of God. All the creation of God is a mir-
ror in which God's glory, pity, sweetness, and goodness
are reflected; and all the creatures are, as it were, a lad-
der of ascent whereby to go up into the heart of God. It
is through His creatures that He speaks to us. We shall
love everything that He has made: the trees of the forest
and the flowers of the field, and the dumb creatures—
they all will be objects of love and kindness because
they are loved of their Maker, and their Maker's hand
is seen upon them.

2. Charity, then, is the first mark. And the second is
liberty, that is, while we love the creatures of God, to
be brought into bondage by none of them. The great sin
of the world is, that it worships and loves the creature
more than the Creator. The great sin of us all is
creature worship, putting creatures in the place of God;
and this brings us into bondage. We lose our liberty.
The creatures darken our understanding, corrupt our
hearts, bias our will, turn us away from the service of
God to serve the world with its ambitions and its prides
and its honors and its fascinations, its covetousness, its
craving, and its servility. There is something sad and

contemptible in the dependence of men upon the breath of the world, the praise of the world, the blame of the world. If you are men that are "risen with Christ," as the Apostle says, "mind the things that are above, not the things on the earth; you are dead, and your life is hid with Christ in God." (*Col.* 3:2-3). Be not brought into bondage to the world.

But there is one creature in the world which is the most subtle of all—there is one creature which is the most fascinating, the most deceitful, and which brings men into bondage more than anything else, and that creature is self—the love of self. The love of self is shown in the violent choosing of our will for this or for that, without wisdom and without reason; setting our hearts upon things until they grow so attached that they grow into them; and if they are taken from us, we think we are wounded to death, as if we had lost a limb; then comes sorrow, disgust, discontent, sadness—which is a possession of the devil, for the "sorrow of this world worketh death" (*2 Cor.* 7:10); and then we rise in rebellion against God.

The Man of Sorrows sorrowed not for Himself, but for us; the true and perfect sympathy of the Man of Sorrows was for others. There are only two centers, God and ourselves; and we must rest on one or on the other. If we rest our full weight upon ourselves, we are not resting so much as the weight of a feather upon God, but simply living in ourselves and for ourselves; and we shall suffer—suffer in this world continual sorrow, crosses, and disappointment; and if we so die, unless keen expiation shall prepare us for the vision of peace, we may forfeit the face of God to all eternity.

Once more: a lot is meted out to every one of us, and God has chosen it. We do not choose our own lot; some few of its details we may control; but we no more choose our entire lot than we determine the country or the century in which we are born. It is the providence of God; and He ordains what we shall have and shall not have; and that lot is given to us: to be content with it, to be satisfied with it, to rejoice in it. More than this, when we see others happier, richer, more gifted than we are, we ought not only to be content with our own lot, but to rejoice for their sakes if they are preferred before us; if they are more loved than we are, if God has bestowed on them greater graces, if He has put them first and put us last, to rejoice in it all. These are the marks of a heart that is living in the joy of the Resurrection. It lives out of itself; and living out of itself, by this unselfish joy, it has a joy in itself which comes from the presence of Jesus Christ; the overflow of His peace, "which passeth all sense" (*Phil.* 4:7), the consciousness of that twofold relationship—His relation to us, our relation to Him, and our mutual and indissoluble love.

3. Lastly: there is one more mark of which I will speak; and that is, a spirit of praise, a spirit of thanksgiving, joy, and praise. We go on praying all our lifetime, craving, clamoring, with sharp and discontented prayers, because we have not what we desire; and when we receive the gifts of God, we, like the lepers, do not turn back to give Him thanks; the spirit of praise is not in us. And yet there will be no prayer of petition for our own needs in Heaven, there will be no such prayer in eternity. There will be perpetual praise; praise will be the work of the blessed, praise will be our joy, praise will be our sweetness forever. If, then, in this life we do not praise God; if praise is not now on our lips nor in our hearts; if, when we repeat the words

of the Psalter, our hearts are earthly and dry, are we training for the praise of the Kingdom of God? Should we know how to sing the canticle of Moses and of the Lamb, who have never learned it here? Remember what praise is. Praise consists in the love of God, in wonder at the goodness of God, in recognition of the gifts of God, in seeing God in all things He gives us, ay, and even in the things that He refuses to us; so as to see our whole life in the light of God; and seeing this, to bless Him, adore Him, and glorify Him: to say, "Holy, holy, holy," in the words of the Seraphim; to say, "Glory be to God in the highest," in the words of the Angels; to say, "Glory be to the Father and to the Son, and to the Holy Ghost"; to say always and in all things, "Thanks be to God." Learn this spirit of praise in all your daily life.

And now I have but one more word to add. Dear brethren, for many long weeks we have been advancing to this day. We have come up from the desert, through the wilderness of sin. We have dwelt on the horrors of mortal sin and on venial sin, on sins of omission, on temptation; we have gone along the way of the Cross; and but the other day we rested on Mount Calvary, gazing upon the Five Sacred Wounds and upon the desolation of the Son of God. Today we have gone up from the sepulcher to the Throne of the Kingdom of the Resurrection; and round about us we may see by faith those whom we shall hereafter see in vision: the Blessed Mother of God, sinless always; the beloved Disciple, who was without spot; Mary Magdalen, stained through and through, now white as snow: there they stand, the type of saints and penitents, in the Kingdom of God, redeemed by the same Lord and Saviour, washed in the same Precious Blood, arrayed in light, the penitent white as the sinless, because sinless forever; for all sins are done away. "These are they which have come out of great tribulations, and have washed their robes and made them white in the blood of the Lamb." (*Apoc.* 7:14).

We have come, then, in joy, with penitents, and with the saints, to the Kingdom of the Resurrection: but we shall have some years still of temptation and buffeting and sorrow and warfare and of the Cross, on earth. These things must be: storms upon the lake, clouds upon the mountain; they are our earthly lot. What matter? If we be children of the Resurrection, Heaven is ours: and Heaven is near; we know not how long, or how soon our day may be. Before Easter next we may be in the light of the Kingdom; or we may be in its outskirts expiating and waiting for the vision of God. What matter, then, a little pain, a little sorrow, a little penance, a few crosses, if after a little while there be an inheritance of eternal joy?

If you have enjoyed this book, make your next selection from among the following...

Prophecy for Today. Edward Connor 3.00
What Will Hell Be Like? St. Alphonsus Liguori ...... .40
A Year with the Saints. Anonymous 5.00
Saint Michael and the Angels. Approved Sources..... 3.50
Dolorous Passion of Our Lord. Anne C. Emmerich... 10.00
Modern Saints—Their Lives & Faces. Ann Ball...... 10.00
Divine Favors Granted to St. Joseph. Pere Binet 3.00
Catechism of the Council of Trent. McHugh/Callan .. 15.00
The Foot of the Cross. Fr. Faber................... 10.00
The Rosary in Action. John Johnson 5.00
Padre Pio—The Stigmatist. Fr. Charles Carty........ 8.50
Why Squander Illness? Frs. Rumble & Carty 1.50
My God, I love Thee! (100 cards). St. Augustine..... 4.00
The Sacred Heart and the Priesthood. de la Touche .. 5.00
Fatima—The Great Sign. Francis Johnston 6.00
Heliotropium—Conformity of Human Will to Divine.. 8.50
St. Rose of Lima. Sister Alphonsus 8.00
Charity for the Suffering Souls. Fr. John Nageleisen .. 10.00
Devotion to the Sacred Heart of Jesus. Verheylezoon . 8.50
St. Catherine Labouré of the Mirac. Medal. Dirvin... 7.50
Who Is Padre Pio? Radio Replies Press............. 1.00
The Incorruptibles. Joan Carroll Cruz 8.00
The Happiness of Heaven. Fr. J. Boudreau.......... 6.00
The Life of Christ. 4 Vols. H.B. Anne C. Emmerich . 67.00
The Life of Christ. 4 Vols. P.B. Anne C. Emmerich .. 40.00
St. Dominic. Sr. Mary Jean Dorcy................. 5.00
Is It a Saint's Name? Fr. William Dunne 1.25
The Precious Blood. Fr. Faber.................... 7.50
The Holy Shroud & Four Visions. Fr. O'Connell..... 1.50
Clean Love in Courtship. Fr. Lawrence Lovasik 1.50
The Prophecies of St. Malachy. Peter Bander........ 3.00
The Prophets and Our Times. Fr. R. G. Culleton..... 6.00
The Life & Glories of St. Joseph. Edward Thompson . 9.00
St. Martin de Porres. Giuliana Cavallini............ 7.00
The Secret of the Rosary. St. Louis De Montfort..... 1.00
The History of Antichrist. Rev. P. Huchede 2.00
Magnificent Prayers. St. Bridget of Sweden.......... 1.00
The Douay-Rheims New Testament. Paperbound 8.00
St. Catherine of Siena. Alice Curtayne 7.50
Where We Got the Bible. Fr. Henry Graham 3.00
Hidden Treasure—Holy Mass. St. Leonard 2.50

At your bookdealer or direct from the publisher.

Prices guaranteed through June 30, 1987.